Acting

Is Believing

Constantin Stanislavski in *The Cherry Orchard*

". . . on the stage truth is what the actor truly believes."

Acting

Is Believing

*A Basic Method
for Beginners*

by Charles McGaw
Associate Professor of Speech and Production Director
The Ohio State University

Foreword by Margo Jones
Managing Director, Dallas Theatre, Inc.

Sketches by Robert Reddy

Holt, Rinehart and Winston
NEW YORK · CHICAGO · SAN FRANCISCO
TORONTO · LONDON

25585-0115

July, 1963

To Fern and Mary

I remember some years ago hearing a very fine and sensitive theatre director say to an actor during rehearsal this statement. . . . "I don't believe you." These words made a deep impression on me.

An actor must believe in order to make his audience believe. Charles McGaw in *Acting Is Believing* has shown that it is possible in a book to put down practical, informative, and inspirational ways and means for a young actor to work toward creating believable characters in the theatre.

All over the world we have young people in schools, colleges, community theatres, and various other working theatre organizations, as well as individuals working alone, who will find in the following pages a suggestion of procedure that will lead without forcing and guide without hindering individuality.

If we are to have significant permanent theatres, we must have fine plays, good direction and production, sound business organization, and talented actors who continuously work at the art of acting with a knowledge of how to work.

Mr. McGaw has provided a handbook of immense value for students, teachers, actors, and directors. This teacher-author's method of suggesting exercises and projects for the actor provides a definite and practical procedure of working. His use of examples from fine plays illustrates his convictions, and the quotations from many talented theatre workers reinforce and illuminate in a helpful way his theme—*Acting Is Believing*.

When we have permanent theatres all over the world presenting fine plays, with talented actors who know how to believe and how to communicate to their audiences this believability which becomes miraculous reality, then we surely will be working toward the creation of a better and happier world.

MARGO JONES

Dallas, Texas
June, 1955

Preface

Although the materials in this book are organized in such a way as to make them practical for classroom use, they are intended for any reader who is interested in a basic approach to the art of acting; and though the book has been written with the stage actor in mind, the methods described may be used as well by the actor in any other field. The basic approach to acting is the same for the proscenium stage, theatre-in-the-round, motion pictures, television, and radio. The differences lie in the differing technical adjustments required by these various mediums.

The approach here presented is based, to a considerable extent, on the methods of Stanislavski. The borrowings have been recognized throughout, and the debt to Stanislavski and to certain of his followers is gratefully acknowledged.

In no sense, however, does the book pretend to be an interpretation of the Stanislavski "system." It attempts only to draw upon some aspects of the system which have proved to be practical in helping beginning actors to develop an effective technique for bringing a character into existence on the stage. In some instances the vocabulary of Stanislavski's translators has been employed. Other terms have been used wherever they seemed to have greater clarity.

Stanislavski's influence has been admittedly great, but the extent of that influence on the modern theatre is difficult to determine. It would seem that his principal contribution consists, not in his having originated a "system," but rather in his detailed analysis and careful setting down of the attitudes and techniques which have been used more or less consciously by fine actors in all periods of theatrical history. Such knowledge as one can obtain of the working methods of great actors of the past indicates that they have always made imaginative use of their own experiences and that they have always striven for truth and a sense of reality in their performances. Furthermore, a study of *all* of the writings of Stanislavski gives ample evidence of his awareness that an actor's characterization must be *theatrically effective* as well as truthfully conceived.

This book is based upon the following assumptions:

1) Although genius in acting may be a quality that defies analysis, the art as it is generally practiced consists of certain basic skills

that may be mastered to some degree by anyone who sincerely wants to do so.

2) Mastery of those skills is much harder and more demanding work than most would-be actors realize.

3) The aspiring actor must recognize that, although rehearsals and performances before an audience are vitally important to his growth, he must also develop his skills through individual practice and effort. Only in this way can he succeed in his aim of becoming a creative artist.

Part I, The Actor and Himself, is intended to help the young actor to develop himself individually. Part II, The Actor and the Play, is intended to help the actor to use his individual creative skills to express the meaning of the play as it has been conceived by the dramatist. Part III, The Actor and the Production, is designed to help the actor in his relations with the director and to aid him in making the necessary adjustments to the technical elements of a theatrical production.

The exercises throughout have been taken directly from modern and classic plays so that the actor may always understand the applicability of the theory he is attempting to put into practice.

The following persons have helped greatly in the preparation of this book: W. Hayes Yeager, John H. McDowell, Roy H. Bowen, Hugh G. Heiland, Glen Wilson, and Dale Kittle.

CHARLES McGAW

Columbus, Ohio
June, 1955

Table of Contents

PART I

The Actor

and Himself

CHAPTER 1

Outside Looking In

It is a commonplace in books on acting that there is an essential difference between acting and the other arts. Whereas the painter works with pigments and canvas, the sculptor with clay and stone, the pianist with keys that control hammers and strings, the actor is his own instrument. He reaches his audience by playing upon his own voice and his own body. The truth of these statements is obvious. The actor's need for a well-trained voice and body is equally obvious. It has been in this direction, therefore—the training of the actor as an instrument—that a good many writers have turned their attention.

Essential as such training is, this external approach may not be substituted for something that is much more fundamental to the actor's development. Certainly a musician is at a disadvantage if he has to perform upon an inferior instrument. An actor is at a similar disadvantage if his muscular and vocal control are not all that they could be. No actor can afford to neglect the training of his voice and body. Such training is necessary to the achievement of effectiveness upon the stage. A fine speaking voice and a well-coordinated body, however, do not in themselves make an actor, any more than possessing a Stradivarius makes a violinist. The importance of the instrument, the *how* by which the artist reaches his audience, cannot be minimized. But before the *how* must come the *what.* The basis of an actor's training is the development of a technique for using his own inner resources to create a character which the playwright has depicted. Creation of character is the primary task of the actor, and his inner resources are his primary consideration as he begins his study.

What inner resources? What does the actor have within that is so important?

Exploring Your Inner Resources

Let us suppose you have been cast in a play and your part requires you to enact the funeral ritual of the natives of Banjermasin. Like most untrained actors, you go to the rehearsal without having given any thought to what you will do when you get there. Your preparation has consisted entirely in visualizing yourself in a storm of applause on opening night, giving ample proof to hundreds of spectators that you "have it in you."

Now what exactly is "in you" that will help you in bringing to life upon the stage a native of Banjermasin engaged in the solemn ritual of disposing of his dead? The chances are ten to one against your ever having heard of the place, to say nothing of your having a familiarity with its customs. Yet here you are at a rehearsal, and your job is to create a definite character in circumstances specified by the dramatist. In all probability you are at least temporarily defeated. You have never been to Banjermasin. You have never read about its burial customs. You do not know what attitude toward death prevails—whether this occasion would be a time of lamentation or one of joy and thanksgiving that the dead has finally been released from the burdens of life. In other words, you can recall nothing from your own experience that you are sure would be truthful to this situation.

What the actor has "in him" is his own experiences. His *inner resources* are everything that he has ever seen and felt and thought. He can use in the creation of a character only what he can understand in terms of his own knowledge and his own feelings. As he is dependent on his voice and his body to *express* what he feels, he is dependent upon the experiences he has accumulated within him to *supply* what he feels.

The need for knowledge and experience in the situation just described is so apparent that no young actor can fail to be aware of it. The need in many other situations, although no less great, is much less obvious.

Let us suppose you have been cast as Romeo or as Juliet, two famous parts in dramatic literature. Here is certainly a splendid chance to prove you "have it in you." Perhaps this time instead of holding your breath, shutting your eyes and taking the plunge, you will begin by taking stock of what you have within you that can help you in creating one of these characters.

Let us suppose further that the scene called for rehearsal is Act III, Scene 5, sometimes referred to as the Second Balcony Scene. Romeo and Juliet are the son and daughter of two powerful and wealthy families which have long been bitter enemies. Having met by chance, they have fallen deeply in love and have married secretly. Within the hour after their marriage, Romeo, involved in an outbreak of the ancient rivalry, has killed Juliet's cousin and has been banished from his native city of Verona. There appears to be no hope of happiness together as Romeo and Juliet say farewell in this scene.

You are excited at the prospect of playing one of the famous lovers. But you must also be aware of the responsibility you have assumed in accepting the part, and perhaps you may be somewhat frightened at the thought of your possible inadequacy. Of course you want to make a brilliant success of this opportunity, but foremost in your mind is the desire to create a character in which you, the other actors, and the audience can *believe*. Only in this way can such an opportunity help you to develop the natural ability you are sure you have. Only in this way can you learn to become a fine actor—a creative artist in your own right.

How shall you begin? Begin by searching for something in the scene which you know from your own experience is true. Begin by asking yourself: What would *I do* if I were in the same situation as Romeo or Juliet? What would *I do* if the man I loved had just killed a dear cousin? What would *I do* if I were banished from my native country after being married only a few hours? What would *I do* if I feared my parents would discover my secret marriage?

The answers to these questions may not be found in Shakespeare's lines, nor in the performance of another actor on the stage or screen; nor can they be given to you by the director. You must find the answers *within* yourself. You must recall your own experiences to discover how your past actions will help you to know what you would do in this situation. You must probe your own character until you know what actions seem right and true.

It is not necessary that you discover at once what your actions would be throughout the entire scene. Determine first what you would do at some particular point; then go on from there. Would you, for instance, want to express your love in close physical contact or would you hold yourself apart, building your courage for the time when you must be alone? Would you want to prolong the joy of being together or would you want to make the farewell brief to lessen the pain of parting? Would you be more concerned with your love or with the danger of the moment?

In finding the answer to these and many other similar questions you will become involved in a process that may be described as an *exploration of yourself*. In finding out what you would do you are beginning to make use of your inner resources and to understand the role in terms of your own experiences. If you discover your actions would be identical with those of the character you are playing, you are truly a "natural" for the part and your task becomes relatively easy. If you discover your actions would be quite different, it is still possible to play the character with truth and sincerity as the dramatist has conceived him. If after a thorough exploratory period you discover that you have no idea what you would do, you are beaten at the beginning and you had best turn in your script. In such a situation, you have no inner resources to draw from in preparing to bring the character to life on the stage. *You cannot play a character which you cannot understand in terms of your own experience.*

> EXERCISE: To illustrate what is meant by your "inner resources" and "understanding a character in terms of your own experience" we have considered the problems of preparing to play a native of Banjermasin or Romeo or Juliet. These problems, involving as they do a specific knowledge of foreign customs or a knowledge of how you would act in a great emotional crisis, are too complex for beginners to use for actual practice. We shall start, therefore, with a simpler exercise in the recall of experience.
>
> In Act II of *The Sea Gull*, by Anton Chekhov, Masha has sat for a long time listening to the conversation of others. She finally rises and hobbles off the stage with the line, "Oh, my foot's gone to sleep."
>
> Here is an acting problem much less complicated than the one from *Romeo and Juliet*. It must be approached, however, from the same direction—*from the outside in*. Again it demonstrates your dependence as an actor on your inner resources. If your foot had never gone to sleep or if you had never observed the behavior of anyone whose foot had gone to sleep (it is often necessary to substitute observation of others for actual experience), it would be impossible for you even to approximate this action. Fortunately, here is a common occurrence. It is relatively easy to recall *what you would do* to restore circulation in such a circumstance. You would probably rise from the chair, discover your foot is asleep as you put your weight down on it, and take five or six painful steps before the numbness is eliminated.
>
> Work on this problem until you can *believe your actions* in connection with it.

Believing Your Actions on the Stage

Several times there have been references to "believing your actions" or to "creating a character in which you can believe." It is necessary for an actor to believe what he is doing, and his first responsibility to his audience is to induce their belief in his actions. So the objective in this exercise from *The Sea Gull* is not to look *as if* your foot is asleep. It is to make yourself *believe* your foot is asleep. Acting is literally a matter of "make-believe." In fact the attitude of a child in his make-believe games is almost identical with the attitude of the actor when he is believing his actions upon the stage.

Children with their mud pies, their kings and queens, their cowboy-and-Indian games impose upon themselves a set of circumstances very similar to those imposed by the dramatist upon the actor. They decide on a situation that stimulates them to action. Then they proceed to act in whatever fashion their experience leads them to think is true to the imposed conditions. The pleasure they receive from the game is in direct proportion to the extent to which they are able to give themselves over to what they are doing—in other words, to the extent they can believe. As the game wears thin and their belief decreases, they invent new circumstances to stimulate them to further action. An imaginative child proposes: "Let's make believe the king wasn't really hurt when he fell off his throne, but was only pretending. He did it so the prince would feel sorry for him and help him fight the Black Knight." Immediately a whole new sequence of action is suggested, and every child enters into the game with renewed belief.

Of course the throne is not real. It is only Father's chair. The king's crown is cardboard. The swords are sticks ("Mother won't let us sharpen the ends because then they would be dangerous"). The child never thinks these things are real. When the game is over, the precious crown that has been guarded so carefully is likely to be kicked to one side of the living-room floor. But while the game is on he believes these "props" are true, and it is a pretty dull adult who can pick up the throne as if it were an ordinary chair and carry it back to the dining room.

Distinguishing Truth from Reality

To understand the nature of believing in a game, as well as the nature of believing on the stage, it is necessary to distinguish between the *real* and the *true*. A standard dictionary provides authority for the distinction.

> *Real:* existent as a thing, state, or quality.
> *True:* conformity to what is real.

By these definitions, the actor's throne and sword are no more *real* than the child's. But they are *true* in that through belief both the actor and the child can bring them into agreement or into harmony with what is real. An actor who believes what he is doing can take a stick and induce the audience to accept it as a dangerous weapon. An actor who is not believing, on the other hand, will express nothing significant even though he is holding the sharpest sword in the world.

Neither the child nor the actor is concerned with reality—with the actualness of the things about him. He knows that the sword, the crown, the throne, and the robes are not actual. He knows, too, that the situation is not real and that he is not really the character he is playing. Toward all of these he maintains the same attitude. Toward all of these unreal factors he says: "I will act as I would if they were real." And his conviction in the truth of his own actions enables him to believe also in the *truth* (not in the *reality*) of his cardboard crown.

Sustaining Belief

Sustaining belief on the stage is difficult. The actor must work in the presence of the audience and amidst all the distractions of a theatrical production. He must be able to repeat his belief whenever he is required to perform. Any doubt as to the truth or rightness of what he or the other actors are doing is likely to upset him immediately. An actor who treats his crown like the cardboard that it really is can destroy the belief of a dozen others, just as a cynical child can destroy the magic of the game by declaring he cannot fight a duel with an "old stick."

The actor may renew a wavering belief, just as the child does, by inventing new circumstances that will provoke new actions. When you find you need stimulation in the exercise from *The Sea Gull*, try introducing inventions such as these:

> You are in the presence of someone you want to impress favorably, and you fear that your foot's being asleep will make him think you clumsy and uncoordinated.

> You have risen to answer a telephone call of great importance and the numbness makes it impossible for you to hurry.

> You have recently been told by a doctor that you may have an incurable disease, the first symptoms of which will be numbness in your feet and legs.

Supplying new circumstances helps to renew the actor's belief because, when he asks the basic question, "What would I do if I were in such a situation?" and when he finds the true answer, he is provided with reasons for new action.

EXERCISES: Here are other acting problems in exploration and belief. Work on each of them. Invent additional circumstances that will stimulate action you can believe. Add new circumstances whenever your belief begins to waver.

1) On a cold winter morning Zenia in *Ethan Frome* (a dramatization by Zoë Akins of Edith Wharton's novel) sits huddled against a wood-burning stove sipping a cup of hot water and inhaling the steam. She is seeking relief from a bad head cold.

2) In *The Weavers*, by Gerhart Hauptmann, Old Baumert, who has not been able to afford decent food for a long time, finally sits down to a dinner of roast meat. His pleasure is brief because the rich meat soon makes him sick.

3) In *Angel Street*, by Patrick Hamilton, Bella takes a dose of nasty-tasting medicine.

4) In *The Late George Apley* (a dramatization by George S. Kaufman of J. P. Marquand's novel) each of the characters returns silently to the drawing room and sits down to relax after having eaten an enormous Thanksgiving dinner.

5) In *The Crucible*, by Arthur Miller, a Puritan farmer named John Proctor returns to his home in the evening, exhausted from having planted crops since daybreak. He puts down his shotgun, pours water, washes his face and hands, and sits down at the table ready to eat his supper.

6) In *Bernardine*, by Mary Chase, Buford "Wormy" Weldy, a member of a high school gang, is invited by an older woman to her luxuriously furnished apartment. He tries to appear experienced, but he is much impressed by his surroundings. He is given a glass of fine sherry, and he has never tasted wine before.

7) In *The Doctor in Spite of Himself*, by Molière, a woodcutter's wife named Martine has just been soundly beaten by her husband. She is trying to ease the pain from the blows as she goes about her household tasks.

8) In *The Enchanted Cottage,* by Arthur Wing Pinero, Major Hilgrove is an army officer who has lost his sight in the war. He visits a charming English cottage for the first time and attempts to familiarize himself with it through the "touch system."

9) In *My Heart's in the Highlands,* by William Saroyan, young Johnny Alexander comes out onto the front porch on a beautiful summer morning. He stretches himself in the sun as he enjoys the warmth and loveliness of the day.

10) In *George Washington Slept Here,* by George S. Kaufman and Moss Hart, Newton sticks his head into the fireplace trying to peer up the flue. He emerges choking and coughing with both eyes closed and his face covered with soot.

Remember the objective in each of these exercises is to induce your own belief in what you are doing, and to induce it whenever you want to with a minimum of preparation and effort. At this stage you are the judge. You are the one who knows when you have succeeded. Do not deceive yourself. Do not be misled, disillusioned, or discouraged by what others may tell you about the effectiveness of your efforts. The effect is not important at this point in the process.

Remember, too, that you are not yet faced with the problem of creating a character. All of these exercises are done in your own person. All of your actions are what you believe *you* would actually do if you were in a similar situation.

GROUP EXERCISES: Following these individual exercises, a problem involving the group may be in order, for the creation of an individual actor must always be conceived in relation to the other characters.

1) *Street Scene,* by Elmer Rice, takes place on the sidewalk in front of a crowded tenement house in New York City. The summer night is stiflingly hot. All of the tenants are hanging out of the windows or sitting in the street. Attention centers on Mrs. Maurrant's windows because it is known that another man is with her while Mr. Maurrant is away.

Working with the group, try to invent related circumstances that will lead to believable action. As an individual actor, you must discover what you would do to make yourself as comfortable as possible in the extreme heat. Clichés such as mopping your brow and fanning yourself are no good unless you can really believe the actions. Merely going through such motions as these will tell the audience only that you are *supposed* to be suffering from the heat. The mechanical execution of such clichés will not induce a genuine belief in your physical state.

Besides the problem of the heat, you must decide what you would do about Mrs. Maurrant's behavior. And what you would do about other circumstances that may be imposed. As one of the group, you must also believe the actions of the others and adjust your own behavior accordingly.

In group exercises it is desirable to *improvise* or to "make up" dialogue which you believe is appropriate or *true* to the situation. As a means to an end, such improvisation may be a valuable part of the actor's training. It aids in developing a set of attitudes which should be maintained during rehearsal and performance of an actual role. Improvisation of dialogue and action requires the actor to *think* about what he is doing and saying, to *watch* and *listen to* what other actors are doing and saying, and constantly to *adapt* his own speech and action to what he sees and hears. These vital activities far too often become a matter of merely remembering lines and action as the actor repeats his part in rehearsal and performance.

2) *George Washington Slept Here* provides another group exercise. The Fuller family, having restored an old farmhouse in Pennsylvania, is entertaining a group of week-end guests. Rainy weather has kept them constantly indoors. On Sunday afternoon everyone sits disconsolately around the living room in bathing suits hoping the weather will clear and permit a little pleasure in an otherwise dreary week end.

3) In *The Blind* (*Les Aveugles*), by Maurice Maeterlinck, a group of blind people are left without guidance in a forest when the priest who has taken them for a walk suddenly falls dead. They helplessly try to find their way out of the wood before an approaching storm.

4) In *Gammer Gurton's Needle*, one of the earliest English farces, the authorship of which has never been definitely determined, Gammer Gurton has lost her needle while sewing a patch on Hodge's breeches. In those days a needle was a rare and greatly prized possession, and the entire village becomes involved in a

search to recover Gammer's loss. Plan an exercise in which the class becomes a group of sixteenth-century villagers searching for the needle. Add a note of actuality by having someone who is not taking part in the exercise hide a needle somewhere on the stage.

5) In *Pygmalion*, by George Bernard Shaw, a group of people leaving a concert are stranded in the rain in front of St. Paul's Cathedral in London. They are trying to protect themselves from the weather, to keep their tempers in check, and to hail taxicabs which prove to be very scarce at night in the rain.

Work on these problems as a group until you have for each exercise a series of actions and dialogue lasting three or four minutes in which every actor is able to believe.

CHAPTER 2

Doing, Not Feeling

Chapter 1 has stressed that, whereas the instrument on which the actor plays is his own voice and body, the artist who plays upon that instrument is the actor's inner self—that self made up of his thoughts and his feelings. It is necessary, therefore, that he be able to make efficient use of his thoughts, and especially of his feelings, when he is preparing and performing a role. Feelings and efficiency seem to be a long way apart. Emotions are often unpredictable and uncontrolled. Yet actors in all periods of theatre history have based their artistry on a practical use of their emotions. A very important part of an actor's training is the development of a technique by means of which he can put his feelings to work.

Such a technique has been anticipated in the exercises concerned with recalling from past experience sensory reactions to heat, fatigue, a sunny summer morning, and so forth. In making use of these reactions in acting situations, we have already learned that recall of sensory experience is of practical value in its own right. It has a still more important function in its auxiliary role of aiding the actor to use his emotions. And emotion, properly directed and controlled, is the actor's principal commodity. His past emotional experiences are an essential part of his inner resources.

An analysis of how an actor makes use of his past experiences as part of a technique for inducing desired emotional responses reveals a process consisting of five steps:

1) the original experience,

2) storing the experience in the memory,

3) recalling the experience with some degree of its original intensity,

4) using the experience as a basis for action,

5) allowing the action to induce the desired emotional response.

An actor may go through these steps almost unconsciously when he is playing a character with whom he can readily identify himself. Such identification means that the actor's background of experience enables him immediately to understand the character's desires and behavior. If the actor were asked to describe the method by which he has created the character, he would have to search his mind to determine exactly what experiences had provided his understanding.

This seemingly instinctive approach, which appears to defy analysis, actually has been the subconscious application of the process of recall. It can, however, easily lead to the belief that the creation of the character has been solely a matter of inspiration. Such an "inspirational method" may on occasion produce admirable results. But inspiration is uncertain, and dependence on it is likely to be a makeshift of the lazy actor. What approach is possible when one is confronted with a character whose actions, either wholly or in part, are not immediately comprehensible?

To answer this question we must examine in more detail each step in the process of recall.

The Original Experience

The original experience may have occurred months or even years before it is recalled and put to practical use. In fact, childhood experiences, because they frequently remain in the mind with particular vividness, are likely to be especially valuable.

An actor's natural talent consists to a large extent in an ability to appreciate the significance of his experiences. The so-called "gifted actor" has an unusual awareness of what is happening to him and to the people around him. He has a superior ability to comprehend the full meaning of everyday happenings. A walk around the block with a friend, a casual encounter with a rival, hearing the siren of an ambulance, taking a trip on a train, hearing taps played by a bugler—all of these are fairly common experiences in which he might find a significance that would serve to fix them in his memory. The actor cannot permit himself to become blasé in his reactions to everyday human experiences.

A common remark to a young actor is "You must suffer before you can play this part." This comment is only another way of saying "Your inner resources are inadequate. You cannot recall experiences which enable you to understand the character you are attempting to play."

Suffering for its own sake, however, is an extravagant and unreliable method of training for the stage. There is no reason to seek involvement in unhappy or sensational occurrences. The inevitable complications of modern living, together with the insight that may be gained from reading great literature and from close observation of others, will provide a sensitive actor with a suitably full background.

Remembering the Experience

Retaining the experience is partly a matter of natural memory, partly a matter of conscious effort. A person who is genuinely aware of what is going on around him is likely to remember what has happened in the past. Any technique, however, which will aid the actor in retaining the details of an experience vividly in mind is definitely worth developing.

This story is told of the great French actor François Joseph Talma (1763–1826), said to have been a favorite of Napoleon and, later, of Louis XVIII. Hearing the news of his father's death, Talma was shocked to the point of uttering a piercing cry. He immediately noted the nature of his grief and commented that the memory of it might be useful to him later on the stage. Such behavior may seem cold-blooded. But there is no reason to doubt that Talma's sorrow was sincere. At any rate, the story illustrates the working method of a great artist in accumulating "inner resources."

Recalling the Experience

In looking for a technique which will enable the actor to rely upon his past experience when subconscious identification fails, we need now to consider what experiences he attempts to recall. He searches his past for those happenings which most nearly parallel those of the character he is playing. They may be identical. They may be far removed. John Barrymore gave this description of recall of past experience in playing the title role in *Peter Ibbetson*, a dramatization of George du Maurier's novel:

> . . . *An actor's performance, at best, is the way he happens to feel about a certain character . . . .*
>
> *I'm a bit of Peter Ibbetson and a bit of Jack Barrymore. At least, I never utterly forget Jack Barrymore—or things he's thought or done —or had done to him. . . .*
>
> *I leave my dressing room to make Peter's first entrance. I am Jack Barrymore—Jack Barrymore smoking a cigarette. But before I make the entrance I have thrown away the cigarette and become more Ibbet-*

son than Barrymore. By the time I am visible to the audience I am Ib-
betson, quite.

That is, you see—I hope to make this clear—on my way to the
entrance I have passed imaginary flunkies and given up my hat and
coat. Peter would have had a hat and coat—naturally; and would have
given them up. And he's a timid fellow. He gives up his imaginary hat
and coat to these imaginary flunkies just as I, Jack Barrymore—and
very timid then—once gave up my hat and coat to flunkies at a great
ball given by Mrs. Astor.

Of course I don't always make Peter's entrance with the memory
of a bashful boy at Mrs. Astor's ball. That would harden the memory
—make it useless. You couldn't keep on conjuring up the same thing.
You have to have different things to get the same emotion . . . .[1]

Barrymore's description is an example of recalling an experience
which is very close to the character. The entrance which he mentions
is Peter Ibbetson's entrance to a great ball given in honor of the
Duchess of Towers. And Peter is a very timid fellow, painfully embarrassed in the presence of duchesses and liveried footmen.

More often than not the actor cannot find in his past so close an
approximation to the experience of the character. Obviously, he cannot have had experiences which parallel those of every character he
might be called upon to play. In such situations he must resort to experiences in which his *desires* were similar to those of the character, although the circumstances which prompted the desires may have been
entirely different.

In playing Macbeth, for instance, an actor must be able to understand Macbeth's vaulting ambition to be king and his willingness to
commit any crime in order to realize his desires. But the actor certainly
will not find in his past any experience which parallels Macbeth's evil
course of action. A young actor's most vivid memory of ambition may
be only having had a desire to play the leading part in a production in
which he had been cast as an extra. His most guilty desire may have
been a vague wish that the leading man would suffer some calamity
which would remove him from the coveted role. Even so, this experience—the momentary wish to realize an ambition at the expense of
someone else—may enable the young actor to understand the terrible
desire that drove Macbeth along his path of blood and crime.

---

[1] Ashton Stevens, *Actorviews* (Chicago: Covici-McGee Company, 1923), pp. 64,
66–67. Copyright, 1923. Quoted in *Actors on Acting*, ed. by Toby Cole and Helen
Krich Chinoy (New York: Crown Publishers, 1949), p. 516.

Another dramatic situation for which the actor is not likely to find a parallel in past experience is the Potion Scene (Act IV, Scene 3) from *Romeo and Juliet*. Secretly married to Romeo, Juliet has been promised by her parents to the Count of Paris. To get herself out of this entanglement, she is about to take a potion which will make her appear to be dead. She will then be placed in the family tomb, and Romeo will come to rescue her.

Juliet's emotion is fear mounting almost to hysteria. She is about to take an action the outcome of which is uncertain and fraught with dreadful possibilities. She is distracted by imagining all the things that might happen to cause her plan to fail. What if the potion doesn't work at all? What if it is a poison? What if she should wake before Romeo comes and find herself alone in the tomb with the remains of all her buried ancestors?

What experience have you had which might enable you to understand the nature of Juliet's fear? Have you ever been in a situation, no matter how dissimilar in its actual circumstances, which induced a feeling akin to Juliet's? Have you ever been alone preparing to take some step the consequences of which were uncertain holding possibilities of danger, unhappiness, pain, discomfort? Have you ever prepared to run away from home? Have you ever contemplated an elopment? Have you ever got ready to go to the hospital for an operation? to go into the army? to go away to college or to move to a new town where you might experience homesickness and have to face problems which you might not be able to solve?

In searching for a past experience which would help you in playing the Potion Scene, you need to find some incident in which you had to control yourself in face of fears that were largely imaginary. Perhaps the incident you can recall most vividly is the common one of childhood fright. It may have happened something like this:

When you were ten years old you went to spend a week end with an aunt who lived alone in a large house with no neighbors near by. On the first evening of your visit, before you had become acquainted with your surroundings, your aunt was called to care for a sick friend. You boasted that you were used to staying alone, and since it was impractical to get a "sitter" on short notice, your aunt reluctantly left you to look after yourself for a couple of hours. You settled down in the living room feeling quite grown up and independent, and looked happily at a picture book for half an hour. Gradually you became uneasy. At home there was always activity and noise. This place was terribly still. At home there were always lights all through the house and everything was bright and cheerful. Here there was a lamp with a green shade in the living room, a lamp with a red globe in the hallway. Both of them together did not drive away the shadows in the large rooms.

Suddenly you were overcome with fear. A noise on the porch started you thinking of thieves and kidnappers. You had no sooner quieted those fears than a noise upstairs started you thinking of ghosts and haunted houses. It seemed impossible to stay on in the house alone. But the outdoors was just as terrifying, and to reach the telephone you had to go down the hall and into the dining room which was completely dark.

If such an incident is your liveliest experience with fear, it will have to serve. If you can recall it vividly, it will serve you very well. Certainly it is better than depending upon some performance you have seen on the stage or screen. At best you would be copying a copy. And who knows how many times that performance has been removed from truth and reality?

Do not attempt directly to recall your feelings. Concentrate on remembering the concrete details of the experience rather than on the emotion itself. Begin by making use of sensory recall. Attempt to remember just as much as you can about the room—the lights with their bright spots, and, more particularly, the dark corners; the reflection of the light on the dark polished surfaces of the furniture; the windows, shiny black in the darkness, reflecting the quiet gloom. Remember the chair you sat on, the objects on the table beside the chair, the pictures you looked at. Recall the odors of the room—lilacs and furniture polish. Recall the stillness and the sounds you heard (or thought you heard).

If you are unfamiliar with this technique, you will be surprised (after you give it an honest trial) how many details you will be able to bring back, and how much the memory of the way things felt and looked and smelled will help you to recapture the essence of the entire experience. For, as we have recognized earlier in the chapter, sensory recall plays an important part in aiding the actor to remember the quality of incidents that have happened in the past.

When you have brought the whole experience back into your consciousness, turn your attention to what you *did* in this situation. How did you deal with the cause of your fear—the frightening shadows, the sounds on the porch, the noise upstairs? Let us suppose that you first pretended you were not afraid and attempted to renew your interest in the pictures. Then you braved your way into one of the dark corners for another book. You tried to reassure yourself by singing as loudly as possible. You went timidly to the window to investigate the sounds on the porch, but could not bring yourself actually to take a good look.

In the process of recalling experience as a technique for believing the behavior of a particular character, what you *did* in the situation is of much greater importance than what you *felt*. The actor consciously concerns himself with *action*, not with *feeling*. We now, then, turn our attention to the fourth step in the process of recall— making use of the remembered experience as a basis for action.

Using the Experience as a Basis for Action

In playing the Potion Scene, the actress has the responsibility of inducing the audience to believe her behavior—that is, to accept her actions as right and true, to understand how a young girl feels when she becomes involved in such a situation, and in some measure to experience the emotion themselves. For an imaginative actress the scene is so attractive that it is almost irresistible. At the same time, it is likely to lead her into one of the commonest of all errors. The temptation of the inexperienced performer is to launch into the famous speech without adequate preparation, working up an extreme muscular tension which she mistakes for emotion, and being afraid all over the stage.

The actor who concentrates upon *being afraid, being angry, being happy, being sad,* or *being anything emotional* is certain to fail. Emotion may be the actor's principal commodity, but he does not concern himself with producing an emotional state. He is concerned instead with the specific cause of the emotion; and he concentrates on dealing with the cause. In other words, he does what he would do *if* he were faced with the same situation in actual life.

When you are angry your mind is not taken up with being angry. You are concerned with the *cause*—the person or the thing that has made you angry. And you may deal with the cause in any one of a variety of ways. You may overlook it. You may find release for your anger in some act of physical violence. You may appear to forgive and actually be plotting some dreadful retaliation. Certainly you are not saying to yourself, "I must be angry." Your attention is directed toward the tricycle that you have just fallen over or toward the person who has placed you in an embarrassing position.

When you are in a frightening situation you do not want to be

afraid. What you want lies in quite the opposite direction—to dispel
your fear in one way or another. You may want to escape from the
situation altogether. You may want to seek comfort from someone.
You may want to calm your fears by turning your attention to something else. You may want to run and hide. You may want to take some
practical steps which will remove the source of danger.

It is in this desire to deal with the cause of the emotion that the
actor finds most help. When he asks himself the question, "What do I
feel?" he can receive help in only the most general terms. But when
he asks himself, "What do I want?" he can find a specific answer which
can in turn lead to positive action.

When you burn your hand, you *feel* pain. But you *want* to relieve
the pain by applying salve, butter, cold water, or whatever remedy may
be available. When a celebrity is pointed out to you in a crowd, you
feel interest or curiosity. But you *want* to get in a position from which
you can see him to good advantage. To concentrate on feeling pain or
curiosity is no help on the stage because it provides you with nothing
to do. To rub salve on a burning hand or to work your way through
a crowd to a vantage point is a great help because it gives you a definite
physical objective.

Positive action arising from a strong desire to deal with the cause
of emotion is the means by which the actor discharges his principal responsibility to the audience—that of inducing them to believe the character he is playing. The audience is convinced by what it sees. We
may go to the theatre to *hear* an opera, but we go to *see* a play. The
old saying "Seeing is believing" is nowhere more applicable than on
the stage.

What holds for the audience holds to an even greater degree for the
actor. His problem of creating a character in which he can *believe* is
to a large extent the problem of finding action which he can accept as
right and true in the light of his own experience and in terms of the
circumstances provided by the dramatist. It is difficult, almost to the
point of impossibility, to walk onto the stage and simply believe that
you are angry or that you are in pain. It is quite possible to believe
the action of kicking the offending tricycle against which you have
just cracked your shins or the action of gently applying salve to a burning hand.

In attempting to discover how the actor may use the recall of
experience as a basis for action, we have made the following observations:

1) The actor cannot feel an emotion *in general.* He directs his attention toward the specific cause of the emotion.

2) Directing his attention toward the cause of the emotion produces strong desires, the exact nature of which will be determined by his background.

3) He attempts to realize these desires through action which seems right and true to the situation in terms of his own experience.

Inducing the Emotional Response

The technique described in Chapter 1 of asking, "What would I *do* if I were in this situation?" is the basic technique for inducing the desired emotional response. A character exists on the stage, both for the actor and for the audience, in what he *does.* The actor arrives at the true feeling of his character by forgetting emotion and turning his attention to the action which he believes the situation requires.

Moreover, in deciding what to do in any given situation, the actor is not concerned with choosing action for the immediate purpose of arousing emotion. Such an approach can lead only to clichés, to stereotyped movements and gestures. The actor must not depend on such stock reactions as clenching his fists to show that he is angry, putting his hand to his forehead to show that he is thoughtful, or contorting the muscles of his face to show that he is in pain.

On the stage, just as in life, a character is angry or thoughtful or in pain because of something that has happened to cause his emotional reaction. On the stage, therefore, the actor is concerned with dealing with what has gone before. He concentrates upon the *cause,* leaving the resulting emotional response to come by itself.

EXERCISES: Following are several situations, taken from plays, which provide opportunity for recalling experiences and also for finding action that is both suitable to the circumstances and believable in terms of the experience that has been recalled. Work on several of these problems. *Improvise* appropriate lines whenever you feel they will help you to believe the situation. At this point do not concern yourself to any extent with characterization. Do the exercises in your own person. In each case:

a) Recall from your past the experience or experiences which will be most helpful to you in understanding the behavior of the character. Remember you are seeking specific incidents in your memory which induced feelings similar to those of the character you are going to perform. The circumstances of the incidents you recall may be entirely different from those in the play.

b) Attempt to bring back your experience with some degree of its original intensity. Concentrate on your *sensory reactions* and on *what you did* in the situation. Do not attempt directly to recapture the emotion.

c) With the truth and awareness of your own experience to guide you, find a series of actions two or three minutes long suitable to the situation on which you are working. Concentrate on using the action to deal with the *cause*, not to produce an emotional *result*.

d) Rehearse the actions until you can *believe* them and until you can repeat them with belief whenever you want to. When your belief begins to falter, introduce new circumstances which will stimulate you to further action.

1) In *The Glass Menagerie*, by Tennessee Williams, Laura Wingfield, an extremely shy girl, is entertaining a "gentleman-caller" at dinner. Laura's mother is anxious for her to impress the young man favorably. Suffering acutely from her shyness, Laura becomes sick at the table. She is forced to retire into the living room where she escapes into a dream world by playing with her collection of tiny glass animals.

2) In *Beggar on Horseback*, by George S. Kaufman and Marc Connelly, Neil, a struggling young composer, is working at the piano orchestrating some music. He must finish the job because he is badly in need of the small fee he will receive. He is desperately tired from overwork and, in addition, he is fighting the effect of a sleeping pill given him by a doctor friend. Finally fatigue and the pill take their effect, and he falls off to sleep.

3) In *Romeo and Juliet* (Act II, Scene 5), Juliet impatiently awaits the return of the Nurse from an errand on which she has gone to bring news from Romeo. Juliet attempts to control her impatience and to rationalize the Nurse's being away so long. Finally the Nurse appears, and Juliet runs eagerly to meet her.

4) In *Hello, Out There*, by William Saroyan, the Young Man paces back and forth inside a cell in a small-town jail where he has been

placed on a false charge of assault. It is night. The jail has been deserted. He is the only prisoner. He is trying to attract the attention of someone who will help him in his plight.

5) In *Watch on the Rhine,* by Lillian Hellman, Elsa, the daughter of a wealthy United States senator and the wife of a leader of an underground movement against the Nazis, has been living in Germany in great privation for a number of years. She returns with her husband and family to the luxurious home she has known as a girl. She enters alone into the living room with its fine comfortable chairs, grand piano, flowers, soft shaded lights. It is a world of beauty and comfort she has not known for a long time.

6) In *Dinner at Eight,* by George S. Kaufman and Edna Ferber, Larry Renault, a former matinee idol, is in desperate circumstances because he has lost his popularity. He commits suicide in his hotel suite for which he is unable to pay the rent. He stuffs the cracks under the doors with articles of clothing. He assures himself that the arrangement of the room and his personal appearance will be dramatically effective when he is discovered. Then he turns on the gas in the gas log.

7) In *Summer and Smoke,* by Tennessee Williams, Alma is an intelligent, tensely sensitive girl who has developed an abnormally reserved attitude toward young men. On an autumn evening she walks in the park realizing that her prudishness has been responsible for her losing a brilliant young doctor with whom she has been deeply in love for a long time. She drinks from the fountain. She quiets her nerves by taking a relaxing pill. When an unknown young man appears, she decides to make up for her past mistakes by attempting to attract his attention.

8) In *The Wild Duck,* by Henrik Ibsen, Hjalmar becomes aware that his young daughter is not carrying on her usual activities in her usual place. He searches for her in great concern because he remembers he has recently made remarks which have hurt the child deeply. A shot is heard from an adjoining room. He goes hurriedly to investigate. He returns carrying the dead body of his daughter.

9) In *The Jewish Wife,* by Bertold Brecht, the scene is Nazi Germany before World War II. A young Jewish woman is packing her bags to leave her home because she realizes her presence is en-

dangering her husband's professional standing. As she packs the various articles she will need, she plans how she will say good-by to her husband.

10) In *The Crucible*, by Arthur Miller, the Reverend Samuel Parris, a Puritan minister, is praying at the bedside of his young daughter Betty. She is suffering from a strange illness and he fears she may have been afflicted by witchcraft. Throughout the village there is widespread concern and curiosity over Betty's condition. As Reverend Parris prays for her recovery, he is forced to keep other people out of the room.

CHAPTER 3

Taking It Easy

Emotion means literally "outward movement." By definition the word implies an "impulse toward open action." The exercises of the first two chapters have been intended to emphasize the importance to the actor of recognizing the true meaning of this word, and of concerning himself with *action* rather than with *feeling*. The question which serves as a springboard to understanding a character is always, "What did I do or what would I do in a similar situation?" The question is never, "How did I feel?" or "How would I feel?"

Already in working on these exercises you must have been confronted with one of the actor's greatest problems—freeing himself from muscular tension and achieving a state of relaxation which will permit him complete freedom of action. This is a difficulty from which an actor is never entirely liberated, because the problem is not a simple matter of self-consciousness which he outgrows as he gains experience. All actors develop more or less conscious techniques of eliminating harmful muscular tension. And harmful tension may be described as more tension than is needed to execute a movement or to maintain a position. Good movement is characterized by economy of muscular tension.

Relaxation is necessary to both the internal and the external aspects of acting. It is much more fundamental to the acting art than the mere facility it provides for gesturing gracefully and moving easily about the stage. Without it the actor cannot give his attention to the subtle process by which a character is brought into existence. He cannot concentrate upon recalling experience, nor concern himself wholeheartedly with the desires of the character he is playing when he is suffering from excessive tension. As Stanislavski points out, it is impossible to multiply thirty-seven times nine while holding up the corner of a piano.[1] The tension of the inexperienced actor is often as great as the tension required to lift a heavy weight. And the problems that demand his concentration are no less complicated than a problem in multiplication.

Relaxation is equally important in the process of realizing the desires of a character in terms of action. When an actor is suffering from muscular tension, it matters little what action his inner state may prompt

---

[1] Constantin Stanislavski, *An Actor Prepares* (New York: Theatre Arts Books, 1936), p. 91.

him to. What the audience sees is his own nervous mannerisms. Instead of seeing the wishes of the character expressed in believable action, the audience sees an externalization of the actor's own desire to relieve his muscular tension. And his nervous mannerisms will be essentially the same regardless of the character or the situation. This sameness is one of the reasons that some actors always seem to play themselves even though they attempt a great variety of characters.

It is generally recognized that physical exercise to develop coordination and muscular control is an essential part of the actor's training. Fencing and some form of dancing are required subjects in many schools of the theatre. They are especially valuable in developing poise and alertness, and besides there is always the possibility of an actor's being required to dance or duel on the stage. Athletic training—particularly swimming, tennis, gymnastics—is highly desirable. Anyone seriously interested in acting will engage in some training program to provide himself with a coordinated and responsive body.

Relaxation, however, is only in part a matter of general conditioning. The advantages gained from physical exercise do not always carry over directly to the stage. Many an athlete whose movement on the tennis court is a model of economy and coordination is awkward almost to the point of paralysis when he attempts a simple assignment in acting. The gallery of spectators watching intently as he serves and returns does not unnerve him in the least. In fact, he is hardly aware of being watched. But a few observers at a rehearsal may make him painfully self-conscious, unable to function as an actor with any degree of ease or effectiveness.

The principal difference between his performance on the tennis court and his performance on the stage lies in the fact that as a tennis player his actions are completely justified. He knows exactly *why* he is doing what he is doing, and he has developed a technique for doing it efficiently. All of his attention is directed toward accomplishing a purpose that seems entirely right and clear. In other words, he forgets himself and concentrates on winning the game. As an actor, he is unable to forget himself because he cannot justify his actions to the extent that they compel his attention. Furthermore he does not have a technique on the stage which gives him confidence in his ability to do what the situation requires of him.

"Forgetting himself on the stage" and "losing himself in the part" are phrases frequently heard to describe a certain state of being that an actor can achieve. To gain freedom from muscular tension the actor must "forget himself," but there is considerable misunderstanding as to what happens when he does. There is a popular notion that when an actor forgets himself he goes into some kind of trance, becomes unaware of his surroundings, surrenders himself to his emotions, and loses control of the situation. Such a state would be undesirable, of course, and fortunately it rarely occurs. A young actor would be unable to achieve it; an experienced actor would not permit it.

"Forgetting himself" means the same thing to the actor as to the athlete. In no sense does it involve loss of control nor anything resembling self-hypnosis. It is rather a condition in which control is at its fullest. It is a state in which the actor is free from (that is, in which he forgets) any anxiety over his own shortcomings or his responsibility to the audience and concerns himself entirely with bringing a character to life on the stage. Worry over what audiences may think of him as an actor or over his responsibility to keep the audience "entertained" is the greatest enemy of relaxation. Stanislavski estimated that this anxiety often produces an excess of muscular tension of as much as 90 per cent. One of his favorite directions, in fact, for getting actors to relax was "Cut out 90 per cent."

The athlete is just as dependent as the actor on the approval of the spectators. Nevertheless, during the game he forgets them and concentrates on winning. That is his purpose. He knows if he accomplishes it by fair means the spectators will be satisfied and will overlook any minor errors or shortcomings of form.

The actor's purpose is to create a believable character. He creates belief for the audience when he creates belief for himself. To accomplish his purpose he must be able to concentrate on it by freeing his mind from worry over nonessentials.

Relaxing through Justification

Freeing oneself from worry over nonessentials is not always an easy task. Elimination of muscular tension cannot be achieved simply by wishing. The advice most frequently given to young actors is "Just relax. Take it easy." The advice is entirely sound, but more often than not it produces exactly the opposite of the desired effect. It is likely to make the actor even more acutely aware of his tension and, consequently, tends to increase it.

The road to relaxation has already been pointed out. Assuming a set of muscles even moderately well coordinated (the well-trained body, of course, provides a definite advantage), undesirable tension is eliminated when the actor becomes absorbed in realizing a desire through action. *Becoming absorbed* means ignoring the *way* he carries out the action. He is not concerned with impressing an audience. He forgets himself as the performer of the action and concentrates entirely upon attaining his end. He gives all his attention to closing the door in order to shut out the noise from the corridor, or to packing his bags in order to escape from his nagging wife.

Such absorption is possible only when the action is logical and purposeful. Action directed toward accomplishing a logical purpose is said to be motivated or *justified*. Justification and concentration are, therefore, the direct means to muscular relaxation. Concentration of attention is the subject of the next chapter. Just now we are concerned with exercises in *justification* which will develop muscular control and eliminate undesirable tension—exercises which will help the actor to follow the direction, "Just relax. Take it easy."

EXERCISES: 1) *Believe* you are picking apples from a tree, the branches of which can be reached only by standing on your toes and extending your arms to their utmost. In order to avoid bruising it, place each apple carefully in a basket on the ground. Make every use you can of sensory recall in order to bring this situation into existence. Again your objective is not to *pretend* you are picking apples. See the tree. See the apples. Feel the apples in your hand. Smell them. See the basket. Feel the weather. Is the day warm and sunny or cold and gray? See the surroundings. Is the tree in a large orchard or a single tree in your back yard?

Supply additional circumstances that will justify the action to an even greater extent. Determine your purpose in picking the apples. Are you hoping to win a prize with them at the state fair? Are you preparing a basket of fruit to take to a sick friend? Has your father forced you to pick a bushel of apples before he will let you take the car?

The justification for this stretching exercise may be varied in any number of ways. Believe you are hanging wall paper, painting the ceiling, putting up window draperies, and so forth.

The purpose of such an exercise is to provide the benefits of straightforward calisthenics, and at the same time provide training in *sensory recall* and *justification* by which the actor can transfer the benefits of calisthenics directly to the stage. Most physical exercises can be made a more valuable part of the actor's training by supplying circumstances that justify the action.

2) Believe you are chopping wood. Use sensory recall and supply circumstances that will justify the action.

3) Household tasks offer further opportunity for exercises in relaxation through justification. Believe you are

waxing the floor,
shaking small throw rugs,
pumping water,
mowing the lawn.

In every case, make use of sensory recall. Smell the wax. Feel it on the rag. Direct your attention toward rubbing the wax into the grain of the wood, then rubbing the surface to get a high polish. Work in a similar way on each of the exercises.

4) Athletics offer additional opportunities. Believe you are

throwing a baseball,
serving a tennis ball,
kicking a football.

Supply imaginary circumstances in each case. Put your whole body into the action. Check yourself constantly to see that all muscles except those needed to perform the action are relaxed.

5) Believe you are a hunter stalking a deer. A soldier marching in a parade. A soldier crawling on his stomach under gunfire.

6) The actor may justify calisthenics or regular setting-up exercises, and thus make them serve a double purpose, by believing he is a boxer training for a comeback or a dancer preparing for a recital. Supplying detailed circumstances for these or similar situations will serve to make the action logical and purposeful.

This kind of exercise in justification and muscular control may be done "in reverse." Such a procedure was a favorite practice of Stanislavski and some of his students.[2] It has special value in helping the actor to eliminate superfluous tension (that is, more tension than is necessary to accomplishing his purpose). It also serves to make him aware of the importance of justification as a means to believing his actions. It is practical as either an individual or a group exercise.

---

[2] See Stanislavski, *op. cit.*, p. 99. See also I. Rapoport, "The Work of the Actor," in *Acting: A Handbook of the Stanislavski Method*, ed. by Toby Cole (New York: Crown Publishers, 1947).

a) Throw yourself into some position entirely at random. The position must be completely unpremeditated. If it turns out to be quite ridiculous, so much the better.

b) Examine yourself without changing your pose. Relax every muscle you can until there is no more tension than is required to maintain the position. (Conscious elimination of tension is not easy. It demands concentration, and you may find as you relax one muscle another tenses in its place. Considerable practice may be necessary before you are entirely successful.)

c) Now *justify* the position. Find some logical reason for maintaining it. As soon as you have convinced yourself that the position has a purpose, a meaningless pose which could not be maintained without self-consciousness immediately becomes right and natural.

d) Make any minor adjustments in the position which will help you to believe it.

Suppose in assuming your random position you crouched low and placed your hands on the floor in front of you. The position is easy from the point of view of conscious relaxation because tension of all the larger muscles is required to maintain it. It may be readily justified by believing you are a sprinter waiting for the starter's gun (see Drawing I).

DRAWING I

Suppose in assuming another position you fall on the floor with your head raised and the upper part of your body supported by your hands and arms. You can relax all muscles except those in your neck, arms, and shoulders. You may justify the position, perhaps, by believing you are a slave begging for mercy before a heartless master (see Drawing II).

The possibilities of this exercise are extensive. It can be made a valuable part of the actor's training.

Another useful exercise in relaxation and muscle control is the creation of a character with a physical deformity. The objective is learning
to transfer muscular tension from one part of the body to another and
to achieve it in different degrees. Create a walk, posture, and gestures

DRAWING II

for the following characters. Concentrate tension in the deformed part
of the body. Relax all other muscles until superfluous tension is eliminated. Check yourself carefully. Have someone else check you.

1) Laura Wingfield in *The Glass Menagerie,* by Tennessee Williams,
is a shy young girl who has separated herself from everyday living
until Mr. Williams says "she is like a piece of her own glass collection, too exquisitely fragile to move from the shelf." Her shyness is caused by the fact that a childhood illness left her crippled.
One leg is slightly shorter than the other and must be worn in a
brace.

2) Clifton Ross in *Two on an Island,* by Elmer Rice, has a club
foot. He is an attractive young man, a highly successful commercial
artist. Imagine a scene in his studio in which he is sketching a model.
He moves back and forth between the easel and the dais posing the
model, making adjustments in the clothing, and so forth.

3) Several famous characters in dramatic literature are hunchbacked. Create an imaginary character with this deformity. Having consciously to maintain tension in the muscles of the back and
shoulders will permit relaxaton of the other muscles. Place the
character in various imaginary situations. Make use of recall of experience to decide how he would act in each circumstance. Plan
several series of actions for this character which you can believe
are right and true.

CHAPTER 4

Keeping Your Mind on Your Business

Concentration was mentioned in Chapter 3 as an important aid to relaxation. It is also the principal means by which the actor controls the attention of his audience. And it may well be said that controlling the attention of the audience is one of the actor's primary objectives. If every person in the audience is hearing what the actor wants him to hear and seeing what the actor wants him to see during every moment of a performance, the actor has gone a long way toward accomplishing his purpose. On the other hand, if the attention of the audience is constantly straying to other points on the stage or in the auditorium, the actor has little chance of success no matter what the other virtues of his performance may be. His chances are even less if members of the audience withdraw altogether to think about personal problems which have no connection with the play.

The audience is likely to be interested in whatever interests the actor. If this statement cannot be accepted without reservation, certainly the reverse is true: the audience is not likely to be interested in what does not interest the actor. *Attention demands attention.* When you are walking down the street and see a large number of people looking up at a high building, you are either very preoccupied or very self-satisfied if you are not curious to find out what is attracting their attention.

Now we have conceived the actor's job to be the creation of a character on the stage in which both he and the audience can believe. Obviously then he should be concentrating his attention on that character. But concentrating attention, like "just relaxing," is easier said than done. Too many young actors are like the man described by Stephen Leacock who jumped on his horse and rode off in all directions. Their attention wanders from what the audience is thinking about them, to what is going on off stage, to what their next lines are, to whether they will be able to get through a difficult scene in the next act, to whether some other actor is going to break up, and so on. It is safe to say that many a student actor never focuses more than 10 per cent of his attention on anything related to the character in which he wants the audience to believe. Thus 90 per cent of his attention is scattered without real control so that it aids neither him nor the audience.

Ability to control attention is essential to the actor. He must be able to concentrate upon the desires of the character he is playing in spite of the presence of the audience, the distraction of backstage activities, and the technical demands of the role. Concentration gives precision and authority to a performance. It is one of the specific skills that an actor must possess, and like any other skill it can be acquired only through hard work and a consciously developed technique.

Finding Where to Concentrate

In developing a technique for concentrating his attention, the actor is immediately faced with the problem of where to concentrate. There is more than one seemingly logical possibility.

The actor has a responsibility to his audience so it might seem that he should focus his attention on the spectators. Such a method would permit him constantly to watch their reactions and constantly to make such adjustments as might seem desirable to gain the fullest extent of their interest. This is the technique of the public speaker by which he informs, convinces, and even moves his listeners.

The purpose of the actor, however, is not the same as the purpose of the speaker. The actor may want to inform or to convince, and certainly to move his audience. But whereas the speaker affects his listeners directly in his own person, the actor affects them indirectly through the character he is playing. In the modern theatre the primary objective is the creation of illusion. The spectators must believe for the moment they are looking not at a platform, but at whatever the stage setting represents—a dining room, a street, a parlor. The actor must make them believe they are listening not to his own ideas, as is the case with the speaker, but to the ideas of the character he is playing. He wants the audience to believe in the existence of that character. Whenever he appears to focus his attention on the audience, he destroys the illusion.

The habit of some beginning actors of looking into the audience is one that must be broken because it is destructive of illusion and belief. It is a practice which has a place only in certain acting styles which should not concern us at this time.

If, then, the actor may not concentrate on the audience, he must find some other objective for his attention. There is a second seemingly logical possibility. The actor must have control of his body and of his voice, the means by which he projects a character. Consequently, it may seem he should concentrate on his physical mechanism. It may seem he should concern himself throughout a performance with gesturing, moving, and speaking with the greatest possible effect and finesse. Such a method might produce an admirably polished performance, but the actor necessarily would appear self-conscious.

We have already recognized the need for a coordinated body and a well-trained voice. But they must serve the actor as a means of creating a character. In the theatre, movement and speech are not ends in themselves. The illusion is destroyed to the extent that the audience is aware of the actor's technique of moving and speaking. Again, except in certain special acting styles, this manner of hindering the illusion is undesirable.

It is not difficult to see where this process of elimination is leading. If the actor does not concentrate his attention primarily on the audience, nor on himself as the performer of a character, the only logical possibility remaining is that he concentrates on the character itself. *Whatever could logically be within the consciousness of the character at any moment of the play should hold the attention of the actor at that moment.* The way in which it is possible for the actor to adjust to the audience, to remember lines, to make effective use of a conscious technique will be considered later when we turn our attention to "playing the part." It is a matter of concentrating on more than one level. On the topmost level and of primary importance is the attention which is concentrated on the desires of the character.

Concentrating on Action

In concentrating on the character he is playing, the actor may direct his attention in any one of several ways, or possibly in more than one way at the same time. We have been much concerned with the importance of action. It has already been mentioned that the actor has the greatest advantage when he can concentrate his attention on *carrying out an action* as a direct means toward realizing a wish of the character.

When Ethan Frome waits outside the meeting house for Mattie Silver, he warms himself against the winter cold by stamping his feet and slapping his arms. Here is an instance in which the actor may concentrate his attention on a physical action. The desire to keep warm in winter weather is common enough, and the action to satisfy it simple enough, that through sensory recall and *concentration of attention* no actor will have difficulty in believing this situation.

In *Life with Mother,* by Howard Lindsay and Russel Crouse, the harassed maid attempting to serve the irate Father Day his breakfast has the interesting problem of concentrating on two actions to satisfy two conflicting desires. She has a wish to discharge her occupational duties and retain her position, but her basic desire is to escape Father's wrath by keeping out of his range. In *A Doll's House*, by Henrik Ibsen, Nora wants to keep her husband from going to the mailbox knowing he will find a letter which may ruin their marriage. She concentrates her attention on dancing a tarantella to keep his mind from his mail as long as possible.

Good plays abound in opportunities for concentrating attention on physical action. Sometimes the action is to satisfy such a simple desire as Ethan's wish to keep warm—sometimes to satisfy a wish such as Nora's, complicated by emotional frustration. When action is not inherent in the situation provided by the dramatist, the actor makes his problem easier if he can find action on which to concentrate that will truly express the desire of the character.

Concentrating on Other Characters

Another way in which the actor directs his attention is toward other characters in the play. He attempts to influence the people with whom he is playing. He yields to or resists their influence in turn. The "connection" established by this process is one of the actor's surest sources of stimulation and one of the most rewarding theatre experiences for the audience. Rapoport calls it "stage inter-influence." He defines it as "the influence of the players on one another under the conditions of an indissoluble inner relationship between them when the least change in the behavior of one inevitably brings with it a corresponding change in the behavior of the other, and vice versa." [1]

Stanislavski wrote: "Infect your partner. Infect the person you are concentrating on. Insinuate yourself into his very soul, and you will find yourself the more infected for doing so. And if you are infected everyone else will be even more infected." [2]

This "character connection" is accomplished through concentra-

---

[1] I. Rapoport, "The Work of the Actor," in *Acting: A Handbook of the Stanislavski Method*, ed. by Toby Cole, p. 56. Copyright, 1947, by Lear Publishers, Inc. Used by permission of Crown Publishers, Inc.

[2] Constantin Stanislavski, *Building a Character* (New York: Theatre Arts Books, 1949), p. 118. Reprinted by permission of the publisher, Theatre Arts Books, 224 West 4th Street, New York 14, New York.

tion. The actor concentrates on behaving and speaking his lines so they will get what his character wants from the other characters in the play. Nora dances to keep Helmer from going to the mailbox. She concentrates on the action of the dance and, at the same time, she is concerned with how the dance is influencing her husband. As she perceives he is thinking of his mail, the tarantella becomes more and more frenzied. A director might do well to instruct the actor playing Helmer to go to the box as soon as Nora's dance failed to hold his attention. In the opening scene of *Romeo and Juliet,* the Capulet servants make faces and "bite their thumbs" at the servants of the Montagues for the purpose of insulting them and inciting them to quarrel. Actors playing the followers of the Capulets should concentrate on making the Montagues mad. They should actually make every effort which is appropriate to the character and situation to provoke the actors playing opposite them to anger.

In *The Winter's Tale,* Hermione pleads with her husband to convince him he is wrong in suspecting her of being unfaithful. She knows her honor and her life depend upon her ability to exert her influence.

Stage inter-influence through lines is of equal importance to interinfluence through action. The actor needs constantly to concentrate on "infecting" the other characters by means of the dialogue. A mere reading of the lines, no matter how intelligent, is only a small part of his responsibility. Almost every line of a play has as its primary purpose to influence a listener—not the listener in the audience but the listener on the stage. The actor must always be vitally concerned with fulfilling this purpose. Expository dialogue obviously for the sole purpose of informing the audience is a mark of inexpert playwriting. It always proves embarrassing to an actor until he can find some reason within his character for giving the information to the character who is listening.

Just a simple "good-morning" does not carry its weight on the stage unless the speaker concentrates on influencing the listener in some way or other. The greeting may "infect" the listener with the most casual indifference, with the deepest love, or with the most intense hate. It may say any one of a dozen things, each intended to produce a different response. It may say for example:

I am in a friendly mood. Let's have a chat.

I got up on the wrong side of the bed. Don't say a word to me.

I am perfectly friendly but in a hurry. Be brief in what you say.

The occasion demands a civil greeting. Don't presume that it means anything more.

In each case the actor concentrates his attention on influencing the listener to give the desired response.

The opening lines of Ibsen's *The Wild Duck* furnish an example both of dialogue designed primarily to inform the audience and dialogue designed to influence the stage listener. The scene is the study in the house of Mr. Werle, a wealthy manufacturer. Sounds of a large dinner party are heard from stage left. At stage right a small door leads to an office where Werle's clerks do copy work. Two servants, Jensen and Pettersen, are straightening the room.

PETTERSEN. (*Lighting a lamp on the mantel-piece, and placing a shade upon it*) Just listen, Jensen; there's the old chap standing up by the table and proposing to Mrs. Sorby's health in a long speech.

JENSEN. (*Bringing down an arm chair*) Is there any truth in what people say, that there's something between them?

PETTERSEN. Goodness knows!

JENSEN. For he's been a great rake in his time.

PETTERSEN. Maybe.

JENSEN. It's in honor of his son that he's giving this dinner, they say.

PETTERSEN. Yes, his son came home yesterday.

JENSEN. I never knew before that Mr. Werle had a son.

PETTERSEN. Oh yes, he has a son. But he's always stopped up there at the Hojdal works. He's not been in town all the years I've been in service here.

ANOTHER WAITER. (*At the door of the other room*) I say, Pettersen, here's an old fellow who—

PETTERSEN. (*Muttering*) Who the devil's here now?

OLD EKDAL *enters from the right. He wears a threadbare cloak with a stand up collar, woolen mittens; in his hands a stick and a fur cap, under his arm a parcel done up in cardboard. He has a reddish-brown, dirty wig, and a small mustache.*

PETTERSEN. (*Going toward him*) Good gracious! What do you want here?

EKDAL. (*In the doorway*) Must absolutely go in the office, Pettersen.

PETTERSEN. The office was closed an hour ago and—

EKDAL. Heard so at the door, my lad. But Graberg's in there still. Be a good fellow, Pettersen, and let me slip in this way. I've been that way before.

PETTERSEN. All right, you can go. (*Opens door*) But mind you leave the proper way, for we've company.

EKDAL. Know that—h'm! Thanks, Pettersen, my lad. Good old friend. Thanks. (*Mutters in a low tone*) Idiot! [3]

The stage inter-influence in the dialogue between Pettersen and Old Ekdal is clear. Ekdal must persuade Pettersen to let him go into the office. Pettersen must keep the disreputable old man from embarrassing the company.

The inter-influence in the passage between the two servants is not inherent in the writing. How does Pettersen want this information to affect Jensen? On what purpose can Jensen concentrate? Here is dia-logue for which the actors must find motives that will engage their attention. Otherwise the scene will not command their interest, and uninterested actors always mean an uninterested audience.

The solution lies in supplying additional circumstances. Let us suppose Pettersen is a talkative old fellow, delightfully scandalized by what goes on in Werle's household, always eager to impress others with his knowledge of the details and with his importance as butler to such a wealthy man. Jensen, a waiter hired only for special occasions, wants to keep Pettersen talking. He is eager to hear the gossip because it gives him a feeling of importance to repeat it when he is working in other houses.

Inter-influence is, of course, two-way influence. The actor concentrates not only on *affecting* the stage listener. He concentrates also on *listening* to the lines that are spoken to him, and on resisting or yielding to the desires of the speaker. The "art of listening" is often mentioned as one of the specific skills required of the actor. The art consists of actually attending to the lines that are being spoken by hearing and respond-ing to them at each rehearsal and performance as if they had never been heard before.

The audience must frequently feel, however, that listening is an art more sung about than practiced. Far too often actors give the impres-sion that no matter what was said to them they would reply with the same memorized line failing even to notice that it was not an appro-priate response. Probably in this particular more than in any other actors do not achieve that quality of spontaneity which William Gillette so aptly called "the illusion of the first time." It is the illusion the actor

---

[3] Henrik Ibsen, *The Wild Duck*, trans. by Eleanor Marx Aveling (Boston: Walter H. Baker and Co.). Copyright, 1890, by John W. Lovell Co.

strives to create that, no matter how long he may have worked upon any scene—no matter how many times he may have rehearsed or performed it, when it happens on the stage it comes to him as an entirely new and fresh experience. The close *connection* established between actors as a result of inter-influence is necessary in creating such an illusion.

An actor may be certain of why a character says a particular line at a particular time, and of what influence he hopes it will have upon the character to whom he says it, only when he understands the desires that motivate the character's behavior throughout the play. Coming to understand this motivating desire is a problem to be by-passed at the moment. The problem will recur in Part II which considers the actor in relation to the play.

Concentrating on Objects or Thoughts

Besides concentrating on action or the other characters, there are two more ways in which the actor may direct his attention. He may concentrate on *objects* or on his *thoughts*. Both may stimulate his imagination and aid him in believing. But both are somewhat limited in their usefulness because concentration upon either must lead to action in order to serve the actor's purpose.

Concentration on an object means that the actor must *look* in the same spontaneous way in which he *listens*. He does not pretend he is looking. He actually inspects the object from the point of view of the character he is playing. He sees there whatever would interest the character, and he makes use of sensory and emotional recall to aid him in believing the object and the purpose for which it is being examined.

In *Angel Street,* by Patrick Hamilton, Inspector Rough of Scotland Yard concentrates his attention on Bella's watch because he suspects it may provide him with a clue to the missing Barlow rubies. Another person may look at a watch only to find out the time; someone else may examine it to determine its value. Bella always looked at the watch with a feeling of sorrow and embarrassment because it had been a present from her husband and it was obviously secondhand.

Lady Macbeth, in the Sleepwalking Scene, concentrates upon her hands and upon the blood her guilty mind imagines to be there. In *The Imaginary Invalid,* by Molière, Argan examines the scroll from which his daughter had been singing a duet with her music teacher who is really her suitor in disguise. Nina, in *The Sea Gull,* concentrates on a dead bird which the despondent Trepleff has placed at her feet as a symbol of her heartless insensitivity to his love. In each case the character concentrates upon the object for a specific purpose, and in each case the concentration leads to action. Indeed, the importance to the actor of finding believable action as a result of concentrating on an object cannot be overemphasized.

The Sleepwalking Scene is one of the greatest in world drama. Lady Macbeth concentrates upon her hands to find out whether evidence of her guilt is really there. Her resulting action is an attempt to rub off the blood which she imagines she sees. If any actor is in doubt about the power of purposeful action to aid him in believing a situation, let him experiment with the Sleepwalking Scene without this traditional action or some imaginative substitute. (It is said that the French actress Rachel attempted to lick off the blood with her tongue instead of rubbing it away.)

Argan examines the parchment to see whether his daughter is deceiving him. He rightly suspects the music teacher is using the scroll as a means of expressing his love. He is duped, however, into believing that it is a clever new device for writing down music, and he immediately shows it to his guests with great pride. Nina looks at the lifeless sea gull with disgust trying to understand why Trepleff has presented her with such an object. It confirms her opinion that Trepleff is boorish and moody, and it leads her to the action of further withdrawal.

Objects then, along with actions and other characters, are legitimate centers of attraction for the actor's attention. An object is brought into existence (whether it be a dummy "prop" or the real article) by examining it for a definite purpose and by making the result of the examination a cause for action.

There remains for consideration the occasion when the actor concentrates upon his *thoughts*. The conventions of the older plays, from the classic period to the end of the nineteenth century, permitted a character to express his thoughts directly to the audience in a soliloquy or an aside. Some of the modern theatrical forms are again adopting similar practices. But the theatre of today is essentially realistic. Ordinarily the actor does not address the audience or talk to himself. Concentrating on his thoughts, therefore, places him in a difficult situation.

The problem is one of finding an external form by which the thoughts may be projected to the audience. We may on rare occasions see an actor standing silent and motionless on the stage absorbed in thought and holding the audience spellbound. He compels attention through an extraordinary power of concentration which enables him to believe the situation in which the character he is playing is involved. But this immobile eloquence cannot endure for long. Even such an actor must translate his thoughts into action in order to maintain our belief as well as his own. And the action must be for the purpose of satisfying some desire of the character. It may not be intended merely to express the character's thoughts to the audience.

The actor who would make himself and the audience believe he is thinking about someone he loves, or about someone he hates, planning some pleasant surprise, or plotting some terrible revenge, is in a difficult spot until he can find some action which he can believe is *true* for the character in this situation. What desires, for instance, that could be satisfied in terms of action might a character have who was in the situation of being far from home thinking longingly about the "old familiar places"?

An example of an actor's having to concentrate upon his thoughts and of using action to induce belief in them occurs in John Van Druten's play *There's Always Juliet*. The situation is a case of love at first meeting between an English girl and an American. With typical British conservatism, the girl is worried when she is left alone to think about her rashness. Thoughts of her love, however, soon dispel her fears, and she exits thinking glowingly of the happy evening she has just spent with the young man.

In this scene, the dramatist supplies suitable action. The girl crosses to the bookshelves, takes down a copy of Shakespeare's plays and reads Juliet's famous lines:

> although I joy in thee,
> I have no joy in this contract tonight:
> It is too rash, too unadvised, too sudden,
> Too like the lightning, which doth cease to be
> Ere one can say "It lightens."

As she dismisses her concern, she places the book back on the shelf. And thinking of her happy evening, she exits humming a tune which has previously been established as a kind of theme song for the international lovers.

There is another example in *Arms and the Man*, by George Bernard Shaw. The character is a romantic young girl named Raina in love with a soldier who has been reported to have performed great deeds of heroism for his country. Alone at night and thinking of "her hero," she takes up his portrait, elevates it as if she were a priestess worshipping a sacred relic. Then she returns it reverently to its place.

Thoughts, like objects, demand the actor's attention as springboards to action.

EXERCISES: The ability to concentrate is partly a matter of natural talent, partly a matter of a consciously developed technique. Any activity that requires concentration of attention, especially in the presence of distracting influences, is excellent discipline for the actor.

1) A person training for the stage needs first to develop his powers of attention through general exercises in concentration. The value from such exercises is derived only when they are practiced regularly over a period of time. No exercise has served its full purpose until it can be done to your complete satisfaction with a minimum of effort. Students of Stanislavski suggest the following kind of activity for developing the actor's ability to concentrate: [4]

a) Read expository material in the presence of a group that constantly tries to interrupt and distract you. Hold yourself responsible afterwards for each detail that you have read.

b) Solve mathematical problems under the same conditions.

c) This exercise provides training in both concentration and memory. With the entire group sitting in a circle, the first person says any word that comes into his head. The second person repeats the word and adds another. The next person repeats the two words and adds a third making sure the words do not constitute a logical sequence. The process continues around and around the circle until no one is able to repeat the entire series.

d) Rapoport describes this next one and calls it the Mirror Exercise. "The two people doing the exercise stand opposite each other; one makes a movement, the other copies him exactly as in a mirror. The director of the group looks on and points out any errors."

2) Find bits from plays which provide opportunity to concentrate on an action, on an object, on a thought. Supplying whatever circumstances are necessary to establish your belief, work out pantomimes

---

[4] See especially Rapoport, *op. cit.*, pp. 37–39.

based on each of the three bits. Improvise lines whenever you feel they will help you in believing the character.

3) Learning to act is an accumulative process. Return to any of the earlier exercises. Decide exactly what should be in your mind (what you should be concentrating on) at each moment. Work until you can repeat the exercise without any feeling of distraction from outside influences, until you are satisfied that every bit of your attention and energy is concentrated toward the creative process of bringing the situation into existence.

4) Here are more situations providing opportunity for work on the problem of concentration. Plan and rehearse a series of actions based upon one of the following situations. Supply additional circumstances that will lead you to believe what you are doing. Decide exactly where you are going to concentrate your attention at each moment.

a) You are visiting an art exhibit, and you accidentally break a valuable antique vase.

b) You are a model posing for a famous painter. He requires you to maintain a difficult pose after you are almost exhausted from fatigue.

c) You are cooking something for breakfast and you burn your hand.

d) You receive a letter from a friend containing a false accusation that makes you angry.

e) You are sitting on a park bench in a strange city feeding crumbs to the pigeons.

f) You are giving a radio talk, and you have a very bad cold.

g) In the midst of a big noisy party you are unexpectedly called to the telephone. You receive word of the sudden death of a very good friend.

h) You are searching your room for a lost article that is very important to you.

i) Late on a very cold winter night you are standing on a street corner waiting for a bus.

j) At a public ceremony, Catherine of Russia was required to open the coffin of her predecessor the Empress Elizabeth who had been dead for six months. She had to remove the imperial crown from the dead woman's head and place it upon her own. You are a young ruler involved in a similar ceremony.

k) You are an archeologist entering alone into the tomb of an Egyptian king. You are the first person to enter there in over 3,000 years.

CHAPTER 5

Believing through Imagination

Imagination! Imagination! I put it first years ago when I was asked what qualities I thought necessary for success upon the stage. And I am still of the same opinion. Imagination, industry, and intelligence—'the three I's'—are all indispensable to the actress, but of these three the greatest is, without any doubt, imagination.[1]

These are the words of Ellen Terry, one of the world's great actresses. Many others have shared her opinion. Mrs. Fiske once wrote,

Most of us would put the imagination first in the actor's equipment. Miss Terry did, and I suppose I should. Knowledge of life, understanding, vision—these, of course, are his strength. By these is his stature to be measured—by these and his imagination.[2]

Laurette Taylor said, "It isn't beauty or personality or magnetism that makes a really great actress. It is imagination. . . ."[3]

Perhaps trying to argue whether imagination is the most important of all qualities to the actor is like trying to decide which of the four wheels is most important to an automobile. Imagination is a necessary quality. No actor can get along without it. *It is only through imagination that the actor is able to find truth in what he does upon the stage.*

Preceding chapters have frequently mentioned the necessity of the actor's supplying circumstances which will stimulate him to action. It is through his imagination that he is able to find these circumstances and to believe them. Laurette Taylor wrote further,

For instance, take the business of dying. . . . You know that you are not dying and the audience knows it, but in your imagination you must

---

[1] *Ellen Terry's Memoirs*, with a preface, notes and additional biographical chapters by Edith Craig and Christopher St. John (New York: G. P. Putnam's Sons, 1932). Reprinted by permission of the publishers.

[2] Minnie Maddern Fiske, *Mrs. Fiske: Her Views on Actors, Acting and the Problems of Production*, as told to Alexander Woollcott (New York: Century Company, 1917). Reprinted by permission of The Viking Press, Inc.

[3] Laurette Taylor, "The Quality You Need Most," *The Green Book Magazine* (April, 1914), pp. 556–562.

*really believe you are. The business of dying becomes actual to you;
also, you compel the audience to believe in you by the very sincerity of
your attitude.*

It is imagination that makes possible this "sincerity." The first chapter stated that the sincerity of the actor in performance is almost identical in quality with the sincerity of the child at play. The noted German
director Max Reinhardt explains the importance of imagination to both
the actor and the child:

*In children's play, the laws of the theatre may be studied in their
most fundamental forms: the décor, the thing requisite, suggested by
what is actually there, transformed through the* sovereign power *of imagination, and yet with the same clear ever-present realization that it is
only play. The actor is in the same case. . . . With children, too, it is
all play, which is carried on in dead earnest, play that requires an audience who will yield themselves silently, and enter attentively into the
game. Well, what do we do? We laugh. Laugh scornfully or sympa-
thetically—at best, we enthusiastically embrace the "little rascal." But
by our excitement and enthusiasm something is instantly brushed away.
We have done what we never do in the theatre, easily as we might. We
have violently broken in upon the middle of the performance; a* magic
spell *has been brutally destroyed.*[4]

Both the child and the actor create a kind of "magic spell" through
their powers of imagination. With the "ever-present realization that it
is only play," both of them use their imaginations to convince themselves that the performance, for the space of time that it endures, is real.
Whereas the child's imagination may enable him to believe temporarily
in the existence of witches, elves, or supermen, the actor's (except on
some few occasions when he may become involved in fantasy) is not
concerned with things so extravagant or delusive.

Imaginings which are the stock and trade of the acting art are those
within the realm of plausibility, concerned always with *truth* although
frequently not with actuality. The quality of the actor's imagination is
not unlike the scientist's in so far as it allows him to see logical relationships which are not apparent to the less imaginative mind. Although
plausibility and logicality may in some measure rule out the fantastic,

---

[4] Max Reinhardt, "The Actor," *The Encyclopaedia Britannica* (Chicago: Encyclopaedia Britannica, Inc., 1929), XXII, 38. Emphasis mine. Reprinted by permission of The Encyclopaedia Britannica.

they do not exclude the unexpected. The person of original imagination is one who sees relationships and has reactions which are *both* unexpected and true.

Acting can serve a legitimate purpose only when it reveals truth. It is most cogent when the truth strikes home to an audience with unexpected significance. We are likely to remain unmoved by truth expressed through the ordinary and the actual because we tend to let the everyday familiar things pass unnoticed. The actor's imagination allows him to abstract the essence of truth from the familiar and the everyday, and give it new form which will command our attention and make us vitally aware of its significance.

Having talked this much about the importance of imagination to the actor, let us consider more specifically how it may be put to use in developing a technique of creative acting. Imagination may seem to be so elusive a part of our endowment that it will fail us altogether if we attempt consciously to put it to work. Since, however, a smoothly functioning imagination is necessary to success in acting, we cannot afford merely to assume that it will function smoothly without any conscious attention. We must try to learn what the acting genius knows by instinct. Imagination serves the actor in three principal ways. It enables him to

a) supply circumstances which will stimulate him to action,

b) believe what he does on the stage,

c) discover truth through observation and analysis.

Observation is the subject of the next chapter. We shall consider here how imagination leads to action, to belief, and, finally, to feeling.

Supplying Imaginary Circumstances

The imagination has been put to work in earlier exercises for the purpose of supplying circumstances that will stimulate action. Out of action come *belief* and *feeling*. These three are a trinity constituting the foundation of creative acting. Imagination is their generating force. The actor begins to act, to believe, and to feel only after his imagination has provided him with a number of concrete pictures of circumstances which excite him into a creative state. These pictures must be appropriate to the theme of the play and applicable to the character he is playing. Otherwise the actor reveals no truth.

The general excitement brought about by the backstage atmosphere

—the grease paint, the call boy, the overture—which some actors find so exhilarating and some few others so distasteful, can of itself produce only a kind of theatricality in which there is no humanity and no real insight into the problems of the character. Such excitement may stimulate the actor to a fine performance if he thoroughly understands the behavior of the character in terms of his own experience, but it may never be substituted for sensibility and specific preparation. The soundness of this warning is obvious when one considers that the theatre conditions under which the actor works are always the same, whereas the demands of the various characters he portrays are always different. Clearly the same stimulation will not serve for both Othello and Hamlet. The possibilities of neither role may be realized by relying upon the excitement of the backstage atmosphere and the intoxicating effect of an audience.

The pictures which the actor's imagination conjures up must be from life experience, not from the theatre. The process by which imagination determines the actor's behavior on the stage is, in fact, very much like the way his behavior is determined in life. Sergei Eisenstein, the renowned Russian film maker and an advocate of the "inner technique," discusses the process in some detail. He is describing how an actor would prepare to play the part of a respected government employee on the point of committing suicide because he has lost a large amount of government money at cards.

I believe it would be almost impossible to find an actor of any training today who in this scene would start by trying to "act the feeling" of a man on the point of suicide. . . . We should compel the appropriate consciousness and the appropriate feeling to take possession of us. . . .

. . . How is this achieved? We have already said that it cannot be done with the "sweating and straining" method. Instead we pursue a path that should be used for all such situations.

What we actually do is to compel our imagination to depict for us a number of concrete pictures or situations appropriate to our theme. The aggregation of the pictures so imagined evokes in us the required emotion, the feeling, understanding and actual experience that we are seeking. . . .

Suppose that a characteristic feature of our embezzler be fear of public opinion. What will terrify him will not be so much the pangs of conscience, a consciousness of his guilt or the burden of his future imprisonment, as it will be "what will people say?"

Our man finding himself in this position, will imagine first of all the terrible consequences of his act in these particular terms.

It will be these imagined consequences and their combinations which will reduce the man to such a degree of despair that he will seek a desperate end.

This is exactly how it takes place in life. Terror resulting from awareness of responsibility initiates his feverish pictures of the consequences. And this host of imagined pictures, reacting on the feelings, increases his terror, reducing the embezzler to the utmost limit of horror and despair.[5]

As Eisenstein points out, the life process which would drive this character to suicide and the creative process which would stimulate him to the same action on the stage are very similar. In life a concrete picture of the circumstances that led him to such foolhardiness would be constantly in his mind. At the same time, the embezzler would be driven to despair by an image of how he would be cast off by his associates when the crime was discovered.

Controlling the Imagination

What occurs spontaneously in life the actor may *will* to happen through his imagination. He may control his imagination voluntarily. Through its powers he is able to bring forth into consciousness the pictures that he needs *whenever he needs them.* If his insight and his own background of experience are adequate to permit him to identify himself with the character he is playing, the pictures which he calls forth through his imagination can be the same in quality, although probably not in intensity, as in actual life.

The imagination is the generator to action, to belief, and to feeling because it is subject to the *will.* It is the way by which the actor can most readily approach the creative state—the state in which he is able to believe what he does on the stage. And some conscious controllable means to belief *is* the most important part of the actor's technique.

The creative process, then, begins with pictures of definite circumstances supplied voluntarily by the imagination. These pictures lead in turn to action, to belief, and to feeling. Again we must recognize that feeling is the end and not the means, that the actor is concerned with

---

[5] Sergei Eisenstein, *The Film Sense*, trans. and ed. by Jay Leyda (New York: Harcourt, Brace and Company, Inc., 1942), p. 42. Reprinted by permission of the publishers.

causes, not with effects. He is like the interior decorator, for instance, who wants to create a beautiful room. The decorator concerns himself with color and fabric, with line and form. He knows they are the means to beauty and that properly controlled they will produce a beautiful effect. He knows he would get nowhere if he tried to create merely an effect of beauty without a specific knowledge of how to use his materials.

The material which the actor uses is a series of specific pictures which stimulate him to action and which his imagination enables him to keep vividly before him. Resorting to a technique of advertising, we may formulate a slogan to state this important principle: *When an actor acts he has a picture in his mind.*

EXERCISES: Plays abound in opportunities in which the actor's imagination may supply pictures that lead to action, to belief, and to feeling. The situation need not by any means be so desperate as one in which an embezzler is driven to suicide. Eisenstein mentioned, you will remember, that he was pointing out a path that should be used for all situations.

Work on several of the situations described below. Allow your imagination to supply pictures which will provide a stimulus for suitable action. The pictures should be definite and detailed, not vague and general. Be prepared to describe specifically the pictures which your imagination calls forth. Using your imagined pictures as a basis, work out a series of actions for one or more of these situations. Improvise dialogue whenever it will help you.

1) In *Life with Mother*, by Howard Lindsay and Russel Crouse, Father Day is faced with the prospect of having to give up his afternoon ride to take tea with Mother and some of her friends. Memory of the pleasure he will be missing, together with a recall of his boredom at other teas and images of the discomfort he is likely to experience at this one, leads him to a violent rejection of Mother's wishes and to a feeling of resentment and indignation.

2) In *Ethan Frome*, Zenia is the kind of person who enjoys being ill. She is constantly complaining of her ailments and nagging her husband to provide medicines which will make her more comfortable in what she insists is her "last illness." She pictures herself as desperately ill. She even sees herself as dead. From such pictures she gains a great deal of pleasure. She especially likes to make Ethan feel guilty for not treating her as well as he should.

Jean-Louis Barrault in *La Répétition; ou L'Amour Puni*

". . . *spontaneity is fertile and fruitful only when based on well digested experience.*"

From Laurette, *by Marguerite Courtney*
(*New York: Rinehart & Company, Inc., 1955*)

Laurette Taylor in *The Glass Menagerie*

*"The imaginative actress builds a picture,
using all her heart and soul and brain."*

Photograph by Vandamm

John Gielgud in *Hamlet*

". . . *all acting should be character-acting* . . ."

Ellen Terry in *Cymbeline*

*"Only a great actor finds the difficulties
of the actor's art infinite."*

3) In *High Tor*, by Maxwell Anderson, Van VanDorn is a young fellow who lives by himself on top of a mountain. He does no regular work. He just enjoys himself. He is engaged to Judith who wants him to live in town and work at a regular job. He refuses because in his mind he pictures the dullness and frustration of being closed up in an office and an apartment without fresh air and sunshine and freedom.

4) In *Riders to the Sea*, by John Millington Synge, Cathleen is an Irish peasant girl. Her brother Michael has been reported drowned. She is opening a small bundle of clothes recovered from a body that has been washed ashore in order to determine whether the clothes are Michael's. She sees the details of her brother's death, and she pictures the intensity of her mother's grief in case the contents of the bundle should confirm her fears. Her sister Nora is with her.

5) In *The Rivals*, by Richard Brinsley Sheridan, Bob Acres is a young country bumpkin. Having come to town to woo the fashionable and romantic Lydia Languish, he is making every effort to improve his appearance and polish his manners. He puts his hair in papers to make it curl and practices complicated dance steps. His imagination provides pictures of the impression his newly acquired elegance will make on the folks at home, and he visualizes as well the fine figure he will make before Miss Languish. His servingman David is astonished at the change.

6) In *She Stoops to Conquer*, by Oliver Goldsmith, Mrs. Hardcastle is the victim of a deception planned by her mischievous son Tony Lumpkin. At night on a country road, she believes she is being confronted by highwaymen. Her imagination calls forth pictures of all manner of dreadful things that might happen to her. She pleads for mercy and tries to protect herself.

7) In *The Taming of the Shrew*, by William Shakespeare, Katherina is the older daughter of a "rich gentleman of Padua" named Baptista. Because of her shrewishness and violent temper, she is unable to get a husband, while her sister Bianca constantly receives offers of marriage. Katherina abuses her sister by tying her hands and rails at her father because she imagines that both of them are against her. She pictures all manner of reasons which lead her to feel sorry for herself and spiteful toward others.

8) In *King Richard II*, by William Shakespeare, the frivolous luxury-loving Richard has been deposed from his throne and imprisoned for his misdeeds. Alone in a dungeon he talks to himself. In his mind he pictures his past glories and his past follies, and attempts to rationalize his present condition.

9) In *The Three Sisters*, by Anton Chekhov, Olga is a schoolteacher frustrated and unhappy in her work. At the opening of the play, she looks out of the window at a beautiful spring day and reminisces with her sisters about happier times when their father was alive. She desperately wants to escape from her present life. She pictures a better way of living either through marriage or through moving to another environment.

10) In *Sicilian Limes*, by Luigi Pirandello, Bonavino is a peasant and an inexpert musician in a country band. Some years ago he was in love with a peasant girl whom he encouraged to study to become a concert singer. The girl is now wealthy and famous. Bonavino has not seen her for a long time. He waits in the drawing room of her hotel suite for her to return from a concert. He is uncomfortable in his strange surroundings. He is tired from travel, and his clothes are soiled and disordered. He remembers the good times they once had together. He tries to picture what the girl will be like now and how she will greet him.

11) Find situations in other plays which will stimulate lines and action through pictures or circumstances supplied by the imagination.

12) Work up a "record act" as an exercise in imagination and belief. Choose a recording by some singer—classical or popular as you prefer. As you listen to the record, practice silently singing the words until you can perfectly synchronize your lip action with the recording. Supply imaginary circumstances under which you are singing. Imagine you are in a crowded concert hall, in an opera, in a church choir, in a night club, or whatever place seems suitable to the type of song. Rehearse until you can believe both the song and the environment. Keep the picture of the circumstances under which you are singing constantly in your mind.

CHAPTER 6

Seeing Things

The great actors of France have long been famous for their ability to dazzle an audience by means of their technical perfection and the incisiveness of their character portrayal. One of the greatest of these French actors was Constant Coquelin, creator of the role of Cyrano de Bergerac. Coquelin once wrote, ". . . it is one of the necessary qualities of an actor to be able to seize and note at once anything that is capable of reproduction on the stage." [1]

This process of "seizing and noting" is a part of the acting art which is generally called *observation*. The ability to make use of his powers of observation is another of the actor's "necessary skills." We are already aware that few actors have within their own personal experience the knowledge to play successfully a wide variety of characters. The actor, therefore, must constantly make use of what he can observe in the world around him. He must, in fact, go further than Coquelin suggests by making it a practice to seize and note not only anything that is capable of reproduction on the stage, but also anything that reveals truth or provides understanding about what may be produced there.

Here are three specific ways in which the actor may put his powers of observation to work:

1) By observing characteristics of human behavior (manners of walking, talking, gesturing, and so forth) which he may reproduce quite literally upon the stage.

2) By observing characteristics, incidents, situations which he may *through his imagination adapt* for use upon the stage.

3) By observing animals, plants, and inanimate objects for the purpose of *abstracting qualities* which may aid him in understanding and believing certain aspects of a character.

All of these ways of observing require imagination. All of them will be explored by means of explanations, illustrations, and exercises.

---

[1] Benoit Constant Coquelin, "Acting and Actors," *Harper's New Monthly Magazine* (May, 1887), pp. 891–909.

Observing People

Let us return to the hypothetical, but entirely possible, production of *Romeo and Juliet* for which we were rehearsing a few chapters ago. Let us suppose you are now cast, not as Juliet or as Romeo, but as Juliet's old nurse. Let us see how *observation* can help us in understanding, and ultimately in believing this character.

What manner of person is Juliet's nurse?

> She is old.
> She is large.
> She is short of breath.
> She is good-natured.
> She likes to tease.
> She loves Juliet.
> She is talkative.
> She likes to put on airs.
> She is bawdy.
> She is an opportunist.
> She is without real moral fiber.

Obviously this role is not a "natural" for the young actor. Although the process of self-exploration will doubtless reveal at least the germ of many of these characteristics within your own experience (indeed, you will never come to believe the character otherwise), here is certainly an acting problem in which your own inner resources will need re-enforcement from without. How can you provide yourself with a complete and true picture of this vulgar, jovial old soul?

A simple answer would be, find some person in your acquaintance who is like this nurse. Observe her carefully. Seize and note the way she rolls from side to side when she walks, the way she pants after any physical exertion, the way she rolls her head and holds in her stomach when she laughs. Copy these mannerisms and practice them until you can reproduce them accurately. Keep practicing until with each reproduction you obtain some inner grasp of the character because you know the external manifestations are right and true.

Unfortunately, you probably do not have among your friends even a reasonable facsimile of Juliet's nurse. You will rarely, in fact, play a character for whom you can find an exact counterpart living in the next block. The process of observation usually consists of piecing together a number of details which have been supplied by a number of different persons and which, very possibly, you have noted at widely different times.

The actor needs continually to be observant of those with whom he comes in contact. The way in which a fellow train passenger smacks his lips to express his approval may be a mannerism exactly suited to the next role you will have to play. The way in which a casual acquaintance smokes a cigarette may reveal a great deal of his character and may provide the observant actor with an understanding of a type of person that he may sometime have to portray upon the stage. So the actor must train himself to observe closely the behavior of those around him, to retain the details within his memory, and to make use of those details when they can help him in developing a particular character.

The material an actor can use in bringing to life such a character as Juliet's nurse is supplied by observation not only during the period in which he is working upon this particular role. Just as the actor trains himself to be aware of his own sensory and emotional experiences and to retain them in memory, so he trains himself to be constantly observant and to retain the details of what he observes. Mannerisms of a talkative landlady, for instance, at whose house you roomed three years ago, might well be vastly helpful in bringing you to a belief of this same quality in the Nurse. Memory of the way a neighbor down the street used to put on airs when she dressed up to go downtown might help you to understand the behavior of the Nurse when Juliet sends her forth to find Romeo. Memory of the way a certain uncle used to tease you when you were a child might help you to appreciate the pleasure the Nurse derives from exasperating Juliet when she returns with Romeo's message.

EXERCISE: Each day during the next week make a special effort to use your powers of observation. Note carefully mannerisms, gestures, ways of walking, talking, eating that seem to reveal character traits. Try to visit a busy railway station, hotel lobby, or some other place where you will have opportunity to observe different types of people. Practice reproducing some of the observed details until you can do them accurately and until you feel you have captured some of the inner quality of the individual. Prepare a short scene for which you supply circumstances leading to action that you believe would be typical of the character you create from your observations.

Adapting Observed Facts through the Imagination

The preceding exercise prescribed that you supply circumstances which would stimulate believable action typical of some person you had observed. Supplying such circumstances involves a high order of imagination, and it leads to the second way in which an actor puts his powers of observation to work—that second way being the adaptation of observed facts to meet the needs of an acting problem. For the literal fact often serves only as a suggester of imaginary circumstances, a spur which promotes the actor to action.

Stanislavski gives a striking illustration of this statement. Walking down the street one day, he observed a forlorn-looking woman wheeling a caged bird in a baby carriage. He knew, of course, nothing of the circumstances surrounding this situation. Very probably the woman was moving into a new apartment. The carriage was a practical means of transporting her pet bird, and her forlornness probably derived only from the fact that moving from one apartment to another is an exhausting job. Stanislavski's imagination, however, supplied other circumstances which provided him with a richer understanding of human experience, as well as a memory which may at some time have been useful in developing a character for the stage.

He adapted the observed fact in this way: The woman was a widowed mother who a short time before had lost her two children. In an effort to dispel her grief, she had directed her affection to the bird, caring for it as if it were a child. Each afternoon she took it for an airing in the carriage exactly as she used to take the children when they were alive.

Such a combination of observed fact and imaginary circumstances is one of the actor's sources of stimulation. It is a positive means of providing definite physical objectives in which he can genuinely believe. Can you see many possibilities for a short scene based upon the incident of the woman and the bird cage? Can you see her bathing the bird, feeding the bird, caressing it, talking to it, getting it ready to go for the ride?

Many questions immediately arise for which your imagination would have to supply the answers before you could work out the details of such a scene.

How old is the woman?

What does she look like?

What kind of place does she live in?

Is she rich or poor?

What kind of bird does she have?

How long have the children been dead?

How did they die?

What is the bird's name?

Is the substitution of the bird only a temporary outlet or does it indicate some permanent mental derangement?

What attitude does the woman have toward friends who see her behavior with the bird?

Having answered these and other questions, can you visualize a series of actions which would bring this character and this situation into existence? Can you concentrate upon realizing these definite physical objectives so that the *action* will lead you to *belief* in the situation and the character, and the belief in turn will produce the desired *emotional state?*

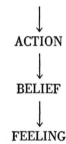

OBSERVATION + IMAGINARY CIRCUMSTANCES

ACTION

BELIEF

FEELING

EXERCISE: 1) Imagine circumstances which might have led to the following *observed facts:*

a) A young man in a dinner jacket walking barefoot down a city street at three o'clock in the afternoon.

b) A sailor in a public ballroom dancing with a kewpie doll.

c) An old woman selling pencils at a street corner and reading a report of the New York Stock Exchange.

d) A dowager driving a limousine with a uniformed maid and chauffeur riding in the rear seat.

e) An old man leading a fawn on a leash down a crowded city street.

2) Continue your careful observations. As soon as you observe a situation which stimulates your imagination, supply a set of circumstances which you can use as the basis for a scene. Remember the purpose of these imaginary circumstances is to provide a cause for action. Action means definite physical objectives showing a pattern of behavior which you can believe might be true of the person you have observed. Work the details out carefully. Rehearse the scene thoroughly until there is no part of it that does not seem exactly right and true *Warning:* Do not attempt to substitute a "made-up" situation for the original observed fact. Without the observed fact you have no way of knowing whether your imaginary circumstances might be true. *Imagination must have a basis in truth.*

Observing Animals and Objects

The study of plants, animals, and inanimate objects as a means of understanding and believing a character is a third way in which an actor may put his powers of observation to work. The process involves the principle of *abstraction*—a principle in art quite generally misunderstood by the layman, but one which for the present purpose may be simply explained and illustrated.

To abstract means literally *to separate, to take away.* The principle of abstraction is applied here by observing an object for the purpose of taking away from it (seizing and noting) such of its qualities as may be useful in developing a character for the stage.

The qualities of elegance, glitter, and aloofness abstracted from a crystal chandelier might well be an important element in coming to understand some of the characters in Restoration drama. The comfortableness, the homeliness, the unpretentiousness of an old leather rocking chair might provide an insight into another character of quite a different kind. The qualities to be abstracted from a gnarled and weather-beaten tree could be an *observed fact* for developing another type of person.

Close observation of an eggplant might be a real help in preparing to play Juliet's nurse. On examining its appearance, one is impressed by its bulky form, its grossness, its unvaried purple surface—seeming to indicate a growth which has matured in size without acquiring any outward signs of character. On feeling it, one becomes aware of its bland smoothness. On cutting it open, one finds the inside to be a yellow-white mass—pliant and spongy—with no core at all.

If an eggplant could walk, it would waddle from side to side; it would have difficulty carrying its bulk about; it would perspire, and fan itself, and gasp for breath. Its bright purple color, symbolic of royalty and dignity, seems pretentious when everything else about it seems to belie those qualities (the Nurse putting on airs before Romeo and his friends). Its smoothness suggests a good nature stemming from a lack of positive principles. Its "corelessness" parallels the Nurse's lack of moral fiber indicated by her inability to understand that one man is not just as good a husband as any other. Her consequent advice to Juliet is that she might as well marry Paris now that Romeo is banished and she may have "no use of him."

As with vegetables so with animals. People are often compared to animals, and in such comparisons the actor may find another application for his powers of observation. We say that a certain young girl is kittenish, that a certain person is clumsy as a bear, that one man is foxy, another wolfish, and that still another is a snake in the grass. These comparisons are examples of observing animals, abstracting their essential qualities, and applying them to some aspects of human behavior. In the motion picture of *The Women,* adapted from the popular play by Clare Boothe, each character was introduced as a different kind of animal. The gossiping, sharp tongued Sylvia Fowler was a cat. The spreading, complacent Edith Potter was a cow. The vicious, husband-snatching Crystal Allen was presented as a panther.

A more famous example of observing the qualities of animals and applying them to dramatic characters is found in Ben Jonson's *Volpone.* The play is a vicious satire on greediness. Each of the characters is appropriately named after some beast of prey. Volpone, or the Fox, is a rich merchant whose ruling passion is greed. But he is also sly, and he has hit upon a scheme of pretending that he is dying so that his equally greedy friends will court his favor with extravagant gifts in the hope of being made his heirs. His friends include Corvino, or Little Crow, who offers his young wife; Corbaccio, or Old Crow, who sniffs at Volpone's body to make sure he is dead; Voltore, or the Vulture, who is exactly what his name implies. Perhaps the most villainous of all is Mosca, or the Fly, who turns the tables on Volpone by trying to prove him legally dead.

Returning once again to *Romeo and Juliet,* let us suppose this time you are cast as Juliet's cousin Tybalt. In this instance, Shakespeare himself gives you a clue which helps you to discover both the internal and external characteristics. Three times in the text Tybalt is compared to an animal! Mercutio first refers to him as "More than prince of cats." Later, in challenging him to a duel, Mercutio addresses him as "Good king of cats," declaring that he means to take one of Tybalt's nine lives. And after Tybalt has mortally wounded him, Mercutio says he is a "dog, a rat, a mouse, a *cat,* to scratch a man to death." With this positive suggestion in the lines, it would be a poor actor indeed who did not investigate to find out what these catlike qualities are that have motivated Mercutio's comparison.

First of all, what is a cat like? Whereas the word *kitten* may connote qualities of playfulness and cuteness, the word *cat* is generally associated with spitefulness, slyness, and malice. A reference to a dictionary will confirm this distinction, and it will tell us that "the cat family (Felidae) includes besides the domestic cat the lion, tiger, leopard, puma, etc." When Mercutio calls Tybalt "king of cats," it is not likely he is thinking of a comfortable household pet. It is much more probable that he is seeing a sleek and slinking black panther.

In this particular species of cat, it is possible to find several characteristics which might greatly stimulate an imaginative actor in his preparation for playing Tybalt:

1) From his very first entrance when he *creeps up behind* Benvolio with the line, "Turn thee, Benvolio, look upon thy death," Tybalt is a *threatening, menacing figure.* Later at the Capulet ball, he is *lurking* among the other guests threatening harm to Romeo. Still later, it is his determination to inflict harm that causes his own death and Romeo's consequent banishment.

2) Mercutio's description of Tybalt's manner of dueling indicates that he is an *expert,* but *unsportsmanlike fighter.* He fights *viciously and inhumanly* by the "book of arithmetic," unwilling to give his opponent any advantage. Thus he was willing to kill Mercutio "under Romeo's arm" as Romeo attempted to come between them.

3) His expertness in dueling would require considerable *grace of movement* and *unusual muscular coordination.*

4) Mercutio's description indicates further that Tybalt was an *extremely elegant creature* possessing a kind of *haughtiness* which did not sit comfortably among the old customs and manners.

An actor assigned to play Tybalt might well spend some of his time studying pictures or visiting a zoo for the purpose of observing the characteristics and behavior of a panther. He could observe the panther's lurking stealth, its leanness, its elegant sleekness, its easy graceful movement, its latent strength and energy, its inhuman green-yellow eyes. Through his imagination he could visualize a person possessing many of these same qualities. And that person, with these definite internal and external characteristics, might be the starting point of belief in Tybalt.

EXERCISE: a) Choose for careful observation either an animal or an inanimate object. Study it carefully. Remember you can observe through all of your senses, not only through your sense of sight. In addition to how the object or the animal looks, consider how it feels to the touch, how it smells, how heavy it is, possibly how it tastes. List all of its characteristic qualities.

b) Plan a short individual scene, either with or without spoken lines, in which you impersonate a character with these qualities. Remember you will not be trying to make yourself believe you are a radish, or an old shoe, or a Shetland pony. You will have *abstracted* the essential qualities from one of these, or some similar object, and through your imagination you will visualize a person with the same characteristics. You will then use your imagination to "supply circumstances" that would require the person to *act* in a typical and revealing manner. Carrying out this action will help you to believe you are a *person with the same characteristics as your chosen animal or inanimate object.*

Suppose, for instance, you have chosen for observation an Airedale puppy. Your list of its essential qualities might include the following:

He is shaggy.
He is cute.
He is playful.
He is friendly.
He is lively.
He is clumsy.
He likes attention.
He likes sympathy.

You might decide a child of ten or twelve years would have many of these same qualities. Plan a series of actions which will lead you to believe you are a playful, friendly, clumsy child. Place your character in various imaginary circumstances, such as

receiving a present unexpectedly,
being left alone and told not to go out of the house,
falling from a tree and hurting his leg.

Determine your behavior in each of these circumstances by observation of the Airedale.

EXERCISE: Find a character in a play in whose development you could readily make use of observations of an object or an animal. Improvise a scene of action true to the character in which the details are based upon qualities of the observed object.

PART II

The Actor

and the Play

CHAPTER 7

Getting into the Part

Throughout the preceding chapters, we have been engaged in discovering a technique by which the actor can use his own resources—his senses and his experiences—in developing a character for the stage. There have been frequent references to the "circumstances supplied by the dramatist" which guide the actor in accomplishing this objective. Attention has been directed to problems arising from certain aspects of specific characters. But we have not yet considered the relationship of the actor to the part as a whole.

Conventional stage terminology classifies parts as either *straight* or *character*. A straight part is one for which the actor is naturally suited as to age, nationality, and physical traits. A character part, on the other hand, necessitates his changing his natural appearance and, usually, his manner of speaking. For the average student actor, Romeo or Juliet or Benvolio would be straight parts. Juliet's nurse or Old Capulet or one of the comic servants, such as Peter or Gregory, would be character parts.

These categories distinguish a role for which the actor must resort to complicated make-up, padding, or dialect, and so forth, from one in which he may look and sound, at least to a large degree, like himself. Obviously, this twofold classification serves some purpose. It is a superficial classification, however, because it is based almost entirely upon external differences of character. And it is a dangerous classification for the actor to take seriously. It may cause him to give undue attention to his physical appearance in a character part, and it is likely to encourage him to neglect physical characteristics in a straight role. In either case, it may lead him to make insufficient preparation of the inner aspects—the motivating desires that determine the behavior of the character he is playing.

In one sense the actor would be wise, and justified, in conceiving of any role he might be called upon to play as a character part. The only part that could literally be straight would be one in which all of the characteristics were identical with those of the actor—a situation that never occurs. Any part requires the actor to *extend* himself, to search outside of himself for understanding and insight.

On the other hand, no part is entirely a character part because to some degree the actor must always "play himself." He can create another person for the stage only by drawing upon his own experiences, actual or vicarious. No matter how much he may alter his outward appearance, no matter how much he may change the sound of his voice, his ability to communicate the essential truth of his role (which is, after all, the core of any characterization) is dependent on what he is able to bring to it from his own inner resources. Even though study and observation in the preparation of a specific role may greatly enlarge these resources, they remain essentially the same as the actor attempts one part after another.

The Actor in the Part

A character living on the stage is a union of the creative talents of the actor and the dramatist. Any argument over which of the two is more important is futile because they are completely interdependent. The actor requires the character created by the dramatist to provide the initial and vital stimulus for his efforts. The dramatist requires the embodiment of the character by the actor to bring his creation to complete fulfillment.

The result of this artistic collaboration is the finished stage performance to which both the actor and the dramatist have made a unique and individual contribution. The result can be neither Shakespeare's Juliet nor a certain actress' Juliet. It must be a certain actress *as* Shakespeare's Juliet. An audience can never see a character on the stage as the dramatist conceived him. They always see whatever truth and significance a particular actor has been able to find in the character. And the person who prefers reading his plays to seeing them is merely substituting his own interpretative abilities for those of the actor.

So the final product is "the actor in the part." It is a unique creation because no other actor can duplicate it. No two actors have the same inner resources. No two actors can find identical truth and significance in a part because they have not had a lifetime of identical experiences.

It is for this reason that two actors may differ so greatly in the same role. The character created has the same father (the dramatist), but a different mother (the actor).[1] It is also for this reason that the

---

[1] See Constantin Stanislavski, *An Actor Prepares* (New York: Theatre Arts Books, 1936), pp. 294–295.

actor becomes a creative artist in his own right without either falsifying or minimizing the creation of the dramatist. John Gielgud's Hamlet is different from that of Laurence Olivier because each actor finds meaning in Shakespeare's Hamlet in light of his own experience. In so doing, each actor is true to Shakespeare and each actor is true to himself.

The discussion and exercises to this point have been directed toward helping the actor to be "true" to himself. It is now in order to consider how he can be "true" to the dramatist.

Discovering the Dramatist's Concept of the Character: The Motivating Force

The foregoing description of "the actor in the part," stressing the originality and uniqueness of the actor's creation, is in no way intended to support a notion that the actor does not have a very great responsibility to the dramatist. On the contrary, one of his most important tasks is to discover what the dramatist intended the character to be. To accomplish this purpose the actor uses every means at his disposal. He familiarizes himself with whatever critical commentary may be available, and in the case of the standard classics he is likely to find a considerable amount of material. He thoroughly discusses the character with his director and with others whose insight and judgment in such a matter inspire his confidence. Most important of all, he *studies the play* to find every suggestion that can help him in understanding any aspect of the character.

In beginning his study of the play, the actor should keep in mind two basic questions for which he must find the answers:

1) What primarily does the character want?
2) What means is he willing to employ to get it?

A certain character, for instance, may want more than anything else to be rich and may be willing to employ any means to satisfy his desire. He may be willing to forego all ordinary pleasures. He may be willing to sacrifice his health and the happiness of his family. He may be willing to break any law—legal or moral—that he finds to be an obstacle in his way. Another character may want more than anything else to be rich, but he may not be willing to employ such means to gain his end. He may not be willing to gamble with the happiness and security of his family. He may not be willing to take advantage of friends and associates who trust him.

A certain character may want more than anything else to find love, and she may be willing to sacrifice her pride and virtue to gain what she wants. Another with the same basic desire may be too proud to make any compromise. Still another may be too shy to let her desire be known.

In the answer to *what a person wants* and *what he is willing to do to get it* lies the key to understanding his character. Here is to be found the *motivating force* behind what a character does and says. And that motivating force is what the actor is most eager to discover as he studies the play! [2]

Failure to understand the force or desire that motivates the behavior of the character means failure to understand the dramatist's intention. This, in turn, means failure to interpret the play truthfully.

Finding a Name for the Motivating Force

Once the actor has been able to form a general idea of "what a character wants," he continues the analyzing process until he understands the character's desire definitely. Then he must state the motivating desire in specific terms.

Finding a name for the motivating force is an important step in creating a character. The name must designate a desire which is true to the author's intention. It must also *stimulate the actor to action*. A motivating force that does not motivate action is worthless.

Stanislavski emphasized the importance of choosing the right name in discussing the problem of playing Argan, the principal character in Molière's *The Imaginary Invalid*. Argan, as the title of the play suggests, is a hypochondriac—a person who suffers from imaginary ailments. Stanislavski wrote,

Our first approach was elementary and we chose the theme "I wish to be sick." But the more effort I put into it and the more successful I was, the more evident it became that we were turning a jolly, satisfying comedy into a pathological tragedy. We soon saw the error of our ways and changed to: "I wish to be thought sick." Then the whole comic side came to the fore and the ground was prepared to show up the way in which

---

[2] For a brief description of how the actors of the Group Theatre used this approach in analyzing a character see Mordecai Gorelik, *New Theatres for Old* (New York: Samuel French, 1947), pp. 169–170.

the charlatans of the medical world exploited the stupid Argan, which was what Molière meant to do.[3]

In so naming Argan's motivating force, Stanislavski was true to Molière's intention. He had also stated a specific desire that could stimulate him to a great deal of action in playing the role. Argan wanted people to think he was sick because the attention he thus received from his family and his physicians gratified his enormous vanity and made him feel important. To satisfy this desire he was willing to become the victim of a horde of unscrupulous doctors. He even proposed to sacrifice his daughter's happiness by marrying her to a simpering affected physician so there would be a medical man in his own household who could attend him constantly.

About playing the hero in Goldoni's *The Mistress of the Inn*, Stanislavski wrote,

. . . we made the mistake of using "I wish to be a misogynist," and we found that the play refused to yield either to humour or action. It was only when I discovered that the hero really loved women and wished only to be accounted a misogynist that I changed to "I wish to do my courting on the sly" and immediately the play came to life.[4]

Besides not being wholly in accord with the dramatist's conception of the character, "I wish to be a misogynist" is not adequately specific to make a good statement of motivating desire. Misogyny means hatred of women. But wanting to hate women is only a general attitude which fails to suggest action. Such statements as "I want to avoid women" or "I want to take advantage of every opportunity to embarrass women" have the virtue of suggesting definite action. For this character, however, they are unacceptable because he did not hate women at all. And what splendid possibilities for action are suggested in such a statement of a motivating desire as "I want to do my courting on the sly."

A good name, then, for the motivating force must be a statement of *a specific desire which the character can attempt to satisfy through definite action.*

---

[3] Constantin Stanislavski, *An Actor Prepares* (New York: Theatre Arts Books, 1936), pp. 257–258. Copyright, 1936, by Theatre Arts, Inc. Reprinted by permission of the publisher, Theatre Arts Books, 224 West 4th Street, New York 14, New York.

[4] Constantin Stanislavski, *An Actor Prepares* (New York: Theatre Arts Books, 1936), p. 258. Copyright, 1936, by Theatre Arts, Inc. Reprinted by permission of the publisher, Theatre Arts Books, 224 West 4th Street, New York 14, New York.

Examples of unsatisfactory statements which cannot motivate specific action are

I want to be unhappy;

I want to hate my neighbor;

I want to be popular.

Examples of better statements which can motivate specific action are

I want to find comfort for my unhappiness at my husband's death by giving all my affection to our child;

I want to ruin my neighbor's reputation in the community;

I want people to think I am generous and witty.

Analyzing the Role

In analyzing a role for the purpose of discovering the motivating desires of a character as the dramatist has conceived him, the actor gives special attention to

what the character does,

what the character says,

what the other characters in the play say about him (always taking into consideration the speaker's purpose in saying it),

what actions are suggested in the character's lines,

what comments and descriptions the playwright offers in the stage directions.

By way of illustration let us analyze the roles of Lomov and Natalya in Anton Chekhov's one-act play *The Proposal.*

The plot of this short farce is very simple. Lomov, a landowner, comes to visit his neighbor Chubukov for the purpose of proposing marriage to Natalya, Chubukov's daughter. Before he can acquaint the lady of his intentions, the two "lovers" get into a violent quarrel over the ownership of a practically worthless piece of property. After the would-be suitor has fled from the house, Natalya discovers the purpose of his visit. In desperation she sends her father to bring him back. Immediately they engage in another pointless quarrel over the relative virtues of their hunting dogs. Lomov faints from indignation and excitement. He is revived and quickly betrothed. The quarrel continues more loudly than ever as the prospective father-in-law calls for champagne with which to toast the "happy couple"!

A study of the role of Lomov reveals a highly interesting character.

What he does:

He comes to his neighbor's house in a state of great excitement.

He frets and worries about his health.

He talks constantly and volubly.

He becomes embarrassed and formal when he attempts to make the proposal.

He quarrels violently about trivial matters.

He abuses his neighbor by calling him names.

He faints from excitement and anger.

He resumes the quarrel with Natalya within a few seconds after he is betrothed to her.

He says that:

He is a nervous excitable person.

He is thirty-five years old.

He does not love Natalya, but he needs a wife to look after him.

He is having chills.

He is having palpitations.

He is fainting.

His arm is coming off.

He is dying.

The other characters say that:

He is dressed in formal clothes with white gloves.

He is a "fool" and a "pup" and he is afraid of his housekeeper. (We must take into consideration that these things are said in the midst of the quarrel.)

He is dead when he faints into the chair.

The dialogue suggests these small actions:

He drinks water to quiet his nerves.

He restores the circulation in his foot when it goes to sleep.

He twitches his eyebrows.

He staggers and faints into a chair.

He kisses Natalya when they are betrothed.

The rather meager comments supplied by the dramatist are

"Ivan Vassilevitch Lomov, a neighbor of Chubukov, a large and hearty, but very suspicious landowner."

"Lomov enters, wearing a dress-jacket and white gloves."

After such an analysis the actor can proceed to "name" the *motivating desire* behind the character's behavior. In this short farce where the characters do not present unusual emotional or psychological complexities the problem is relatively simple. Even so, the actor must take pains to state the motivating desire specifically and in terms that will stimulate him to action.

Since very early in the play Lomov declares that he has come to propose to his neighbor's daughter, we might suppose his motivating desire to be "I want to court Natalya." We soon see how wrong such a statement would be. Before he has exchanged half a dozen words with Natalya, they are quarreling heatedly about the land. And courtship seems to be the last thing in his mind.

Since he constantly frets about his health and his delicate nerves, we might suppose that his motivating desire could be stated as "I want to protect my nervous system from all disturbing influences." But again, even though he does worry about upsetting his nerves, he is much more concerned with winning the argument.

Here, in fact, is the desire that motivates his actions. He is willing to sacrifice both his need for a wife and his need to protect his nerves to the winning of a quarrel over a triviality. The strongest factor influencing his behavior is his egotism. We may state Lomov's motivating desire then as "I want to destroy anything that challenges my ego."

A similar analysis of Natalya reveals that she is twenty-five years old, an efficient person who gives the orders and manages the workers on her father's farm. She enters wearing an apron and house dress because she has been "shelling peas for drying." That she would like to have a husband is shown in her desperation when she learns that the quarrel over the land has kept Lomov from proposing. But she too is a headstrong egotist. She too is less concerned with romance than with standing up for her rights and in defending her dog when someone chances to belittle him. In spite of different character traits, Natalya and Lomov are motivated by the same desire. They both want to maintain their egos. Neither will give in one bit to the other. Therein lies the conflict (and the humor) of the play.

EXERCISE: Choose one of the parts from Tennessee Williams' *The Long Stay Cut Short, or The Unsatisfactory Supper,* which is included in this volume, or select a major role from any standard one-act or full length play. Make a detailed analysis of the character. State the character's motivating desire in terms which are true to the dramatist's conception and which could stimulate you to action in playing the part.

Among the many plays which contain interesting characters for study and analysis are the following:

Anton Chekhov: *The Sea Gull*
John Galsworthy: *Escape*
Lillian Hellman: *The Little Foxes*
Henrik Ibsen: *The Wild Duck*
Clifford Odets: *Golden Boy*
Eugene O'Neill: *Anna Christie*
Luigi Pirandello: *Right You Are If You Think You Are*
George Bernard Shaw: *Captain Brassbound's Conversion*
Robert Sherwood: *The Petrified Forest*
Tennessee Williams: *The Glass Menagerie*

CHAPTER 8

Getting into Character

At this point we have reached a crucial stage in our efforts to understand the creative process of acting. Earlier chapters have been concerned with how the actor uses his inner resources. In the previous chapter we were concerned with how he discovers the dramatist's concept of the character, and how he states this concept in terms of a specific motivating desire. The crucial stage at which we have now arrived is the point at which the actor uses the techniques he has been developing for the purpose of creating a character as specified by the dramatist. In other words, the actor is now faced with the problem of characterization.

Doing a Little at a Time

The problem of characterization is not a simple one. The most common error in approaching it is the attempt to create the whole character at once, to grasp the character with all of its subtleties and complexities from the very beginning. In so doing, the actor is like a starving man who attempts to cram whole handfuls of food into his mouth, instead of taking bite-sized morsels which he can easily chew and swallow.

Equipped with a technique for exploring his inner resources and informed of the motivating desire of the character he is preparing to play, the actor will find his best approach is to choose out of the entire part the single action which he can most readily believe. It may or may not be the first action the character performs. It may or may not be a particularly important action. But to serve its purpose, it must be an action which the actor can believe is true both to the dramatist's intention and to his own experience. To help the actor approach the problem of characterization in this way, some directors rehearse a play in "unchronological order." That is, they begin, not necessarily with the first scene, but with whatever scene in the play allows the actors most easily to believe the actions of the characters.

Having chosen some small detail, the actor must learn to perform the action believably and to relate it to the character's motivating desire. Let us suppose you are preparing to play Lomov in *The Proposal*. The action you have chosen is Lomov's attempt to ask Natalya to marry him —an ill-fated attempt, to be sure, because it brings about the quarrel over the land. But at the moment Lomov is concerned only with making a favorable impression upon Natalya so she will accept him in marriage. Here is an action for which any actor can recall a corresponding, if not an identical, situation from his own experience. If he has not actually proposed, he has imagined himself doing it. Or certainly he has attempted to present himself in a favorable light as a preliminary to asking some request.

The embarrassment attending this kind of situation is readily comprehensible. There is always the possibility that the request will not be granted. And since a proposal of marriage may not be made in a casual manner (lest the lady suspect some lack of seriousness), there is no alternative to risking a blow to one's ego. In Lomov's case, we must remember that the wish to assert his ego is his motivating desire. He would, therefore, be particularly cautious in exposing himself to the embarrassment of a refusal; and he would be particularly self-important in his effort to make an impression which would prevent his being refused.

The actor now proceeds to recall his own experiences in similar situations as a guide to how he would behave in this one. But something new has been added to the exercises in recall from the earlier chapters. Now the actor must behave, not as he himself would behave, but as Lomov behaves. He cannot ask merely: *"If* I were in this situation, what would *I do?"* He must now ask: *"If* I were *Lomov* in this situation what would I do?"* His answer to the question depends in part upon what the dramatist gives him in the play and in part upon his own imagination.

From the lines we are able to learn that Lomov's method of impressing Natalya takes the form of dwelling upon the closeness and the long duration of the friendship between their families. We learn also that his nervous embarrassment leaves him shivering with a chill. Here then are two details supplied by Chekhov himself to help the actor in the problem of characterization.

Supplying an Imaginary Background

Whereas the dramatist provides enough detail for the actor to understand the motivating desire and the essential traits of a character, it is almost always necessary for the actor to supply an imaginary background to round out the essentials that the dramatist has given.

In playing this part, for instance, the actor needs to know what the relationship between Lomov and Natalya has been in the past. Lomov states that since childhood he has had the privilege of knowing Natalya's family. We also know that he is ten years older than Natalya. So he has apparently known her all her life, and we may imagine that in years past he has frequently suffered from her treatment of him. Since Lomov constantly frets about his health, he has probably always pampered himself, avoided strenuous activity, and blamed his shortcomings upon his "delicate constitution." Natalya, on the other hand, in the directness with which she receives Lomov and in the efficiency with which she manages her father's land, gives evidence of being a healthy energetic person. She is probably the kind who in her youth would have taken great pleasure in dominating and ridiculing a hypochondriac like Lomov.

As a result of her attitude, it might well be that Lomov developed a fear of Natalya's ridicule which now makes him more than usually aggressive in her presence. It might also be for this reason that he has dressed so formally and comes to make his proposal in evening clothes, complete with white gloves. He may have felt that the elegance of his attire could not fail to impress Natalya and to compensate for the disadvantage at which he appeared before her when he was younger.

The evening clothes provide further opportunity for imagined circumstances. The remarks of both Natalya and her father make clear that formal evening dress is not the customary attire in their society for neighborly calls. That fact is further emphasized by Natalya's receiving Lomov in a house dress and apron. We may well imagine that he wears his evening clothes rarely and that he is extremely ill at ease in them. The narrow shoes probably pinch his feet. The starched collar probably chokes him. The tight coat hampers his arm movements. We may supply still more background by supposing Lomov bought the clothes quite a few years ago to wear at a reception for some visiting government officials. His are the only formal evening clothes in the neighborhood. He is very proud of them in spite of the fact that they are out of date and that he has gained weight since he bought them.

Characterizing through Externals

This discussion of Lomov's evening clothes brings us to a consideration of the place of "externals" in characterization. "Externals" are exactly what the term implies. They are manifestations of character which the audience *sees* and, in the case of departures from the actor's natural speech, *hears*. Externals are costumes; make-up; wigs; padding; dialects; foreign accents; and hand properties such as fans, pipes, canes, snuffboxes, cigarette holders. The term also includes physical attributes such as posture, a manner of walking or sitting, a distinctive gesture, or any such physical abnormality as being lame or hunchbacked.

"Externalizing" a character is one of the actor's important responsibilities. We have already noted that the audience believes what it sees. The actor, then, must find outward forms which will aid the audience in believing the character he is playing.

Externals may also be of great help to the actor in believing a character. It is, in fact, one of the general shortcomings of inexperienced actors that they make so little use of them. A skillful performance will always give evidence of considerable imagination in finding outward forms to express inner character traits. And these outward forms are often a vital element in the actor's belief.

An especially erect posture, with chin held high and nostrils pinched as if constantly trying to locate a slightly offensive odor, might aid an actress in her characterization of the overpowering Lady Bracknell in *The Importance of Being Earnest*, by Oscar Wilde. A mannerism of sucking his teeth might help an actor in believing the vulgarity of Mr. Burgess in George Bernard Shaw's *Candida*. The use of thick-lensed glasses expressing extreme shortsightedness might help in creating the meek and miserable Mr. Fishkin in William Saroyan's *Jim Dandy*.

If Lomov's evening clothes give the actor a sense of self-importance and make him feel that more than ever he must stand up for his rights, he is making proper use of an external to help him in believing the character. He might well make further use of externals in imagining that Lomov is fat. Chekhov describes him as "large," and it is likely that as a result of his "poor health" he takes little exercise. The excess weight with an accompanying shortness of breath, further aggravated by his tight starched collar, might well help an actor in believing Lomov's rage at Natalya's obstinacy.

An example of imaginative use of externals occurred in a recent university production of *The Wild Duck*. The student actor playing Gregers Werle sought some external means of helping him believe the warped unhealthy state of Gregers' mind and soul. Since Gregers' mind is warped, the actor decided to warp his body also and to play him as a hunchback. The parallel, of course, is obvious. A highly skilled professional probably would not feel the need of such a device. But it helped the student to believe in Gregers' abnormality, in his hatred of his father with his compromising attitudes, and in his fanatical desire to lift his friend Hjalmar "above" normal people who accept compromises and depend for their happiness upon lies and illusions.

In finding as many ways as possible to use externals as a means to characterization, the actor must observe two cautions:

1) He must beware of using clichés, the stereotyped mannerisms or properties which because they have been so frequently repeated would occur immediately to even an unimaginative mind. A lorgnette to characterize the grand dame, dark glasses and a long cigarette holder for the debutante, a Brooklyn accent for the gangster are clichés which are best avoided. For the audience they no longer express individuality, but only general types. For the actor they are likely to mean an imitation of an imitation. They can be especially dangerous because they tempt him to resort to worn-out devices that he can execute mechanically. Consequently, they are powerless to aid him in believing the character.

2) He must be sure that the externalization either *results from* or *leads to* a specific need which he can relate to the character's motivating desire. Lomov's evening clothes make him feel important and result directly from his desire to maintain his ego. Gregers' deformity sets him apart from others and leads directly to his intolerance of their moral shortcomings. Every external must be *justified* in terms of the motivating desire.

Relating Details to the Motivating Desire

What has just been said about the necessity of relating externals to the motivating desire may be repeated with equal emphasis for all aspects of the characterization. Everything the actor does or says or wears upon the stage should in some way be directed toward helping the character "get what he wants." The more clearly the actor understands the way a particular detail will help the character accomplish his objective, the more significant the detail will be both for himself and for the audience. Lomov's poor health, his delicate nerves, his evening clothes all help him to realize his basic wish. They all serve to make him an object of attention and, consequently, to inflate his ego. His fatness and his shortness of breath are the *direct results* of his habit of pampering himself because of his poor health and delicate nerves.

The motivating desire is the unifying factor which guides the actor in selecting the details he will use in developing his character. Anything

that does not help him to realize the desire, or does not result directly
from it, is extraneous. It should not be permitted.

Not only should the actor avoid introducing what might be contrary to the character's basic wish. He should also be wary of details
which are merely *neutral*, that is, details which perhaps do not hinder,
but which, on the other hand, bear no inherent relationship to the motivating desire. Neutral items of characterization are so much deadwood.
They constitute excess weight from which the actor receives no benefit.
Whether he wears a slouch hat or a homburg in a particular part, whether
his socks are plain-colored or striped, whether he gulps his coffee or
sips it slowly should all be determined by the motivating force behind
the character's actions. The way an actress combs her hair for a certain
role, the way she sits on a sofa, the way she says "Good morning" should
all be designed to help her believe the character she is playing. Every
detail should make a positive contribution to the total characterization.

Expanding the Characterization

Once the actor has sufficient insight into a character to perform a simple
action with truth and sincerity, he is ready to proceed to a second action
which may have appeared more difficult in the beginning.

Let us assume you have arrived at that point in preparing the role
of Lomov. The second action on which you choose to concentrate might
be at the opening of the play where Lomov greets Natalya's father and
tells him of his intention of proposing.

All of the imaginary background we have already supplied will, of
course, help in believing this action. But we must now supplement it
with details of the relationship between Lomov and his future father-
in-law. We already know they are neighbors of long standing. The play
provides three other bits of information:

1) Chubukov says that he is twice Lomov's age which suggests he
would expect to be treated with respect if for no other reason than
his seniority.

2) Lomov says that Chubukov has granted him favors on several
previous occasions which suggests that in some manner he may be
in Chubukov's debt.

3) Chubukov mistakenly assumes Lomov has come to borrow
money which suggests Chubukov is the wealthier of the two.

All of these circumstances place Lomov in a position in which he would have to make a particular effort to assert his self-importance. At the same time he would be under the nervous strain of establishing properly cordial relations with Natalya's father. By supplying imaginary details as to the nature of the favors Lomov has received from Chubukov and filling in other additional circumstances from the past, you will be able to induce a belief in this second unit of action.

You might next explore the moment of Lomov's surprised indignation when Natalya challenges him about the ownership of the land, then his exasperation when he offers to make her a present of it, and so on through the play.

Seeing a Part as a Series of Actions

Finding, one by one, the numerous specific actions which when taken together constitute the entire part is one of the most important steps in an actor's preparation for playing a role. He must discover that his part is made up of a series of actions each one of which is carried on to satisfy a definite desire of the character, and each one of which has a definite relation to the basic wish which motivates the character's entire behavior. Harold Clurman calls these single actions "the play's beats," and he says,

> The analysis of the play's beats, the characters' actions, can and should be made before the actual staging of the play is begun. The actors derive a basic direction from such an analysis and from the notation of the beats in their part-books, a guiding line that is the foundation of their entire work in the play. Without such groundwork, we get a display of "general emotion" but not the meaning of the play. . . . The actor's talent becomes evident in the manner in which he carries out these actions. But talent or not, they must be clearly presented for the play to become an intelligible, coherent whole.[1]

What Harold Clurman calls "beats" Stanislavski calls "units" of action.[2] He also stresses the necessity of an actor's seeing his entire

---

[1] Harold Clurman, "The Principles of Interpretation," in John Gassner, ed., *Producing the Play* (New York: The Dryden Press, 1941), p. 287. Copyright, 1941. Emphasis mine. Reprinted by special permission of John Gassner and The Dryden Press.

[2] Constantin Stanislavski, *An Actor Prepares* (New York: Theatre Arts Books, 1936), pp. 105–110.

part as made up of a series of such units. As soon as one action serves its purpose in satisfying a particular desire, another desire arises which must be satisfied through another action, thus leading the actor forward into a new "unit" or "beat." Or sometimes a unit is interrupted, and circumstances created in the play literally shove an actor into a new beat *before* the action of the old one has been completed. This movement from one action to the next provides the *basic direction* (Clurman) or the *through-line* (Stanislavski) which guides the actor throughout the play.

Again, *The Proposal* will provide an illustration. Here is a list of the units of action that will provide a basic direction to an actor playing Lomov from the beginning of the play to his first exit:

1) He greets Chubukov, Natalya's father. His action here is *to get the father's approval for his proposal.*

2) Left alone, he wonders about the wisdom of making such a proposal. His action here is *to rationalize what he is doing.*

3) Natalya enters, and his action is *to get her to consent to marry him.*

4) Before he can satisfy this desire, Natalya challenges his ownership of Oxen Meadows. His new action is *to stand up for his rights.*

5) The quarrel degenerates into name-calling. His action is *to insult Natalya and her father.*

6) The strain of the quarrel taxes his "delicate constitution." His action is *to protect his health.*

In analyzing the role of Natalya, we discover the following units of action in the first section of the play:

1) She receives Lomov in a friendly but rather conventional manner. Certainly she has no notion that a proposal of marriage is forthcoming. Her action is *to discharge her social duties in receiving a neighborly call.*

2) Lomov refers to Oxen Meadows as belonging to him, and immediately she becomes indignant. Her action is *to set Lomov straight for being so presumptuous.*

3) As the quarrel progresses, she, too, starts calling names. Her action is *to insult Lomov.*

4) After Lomov leaves and she discovers he had come to make

a marriage proposal, she is almost overcome at the thought of having lost a husband. Her action is *to get her father to get Lomov back.*

And so on through the play.

Characterization, then, is a process of breaking a role into a series of small actions and inducing a belief in each of them by proceeding from the less difficult to the more difficult. It is an exciting and an exacting process. The actor who approaches the problem of characterization with the attitude that "there is nothing to it" is certain to achieve, at best, only a part of his potential success. There are few actors, even of the highest professional caliber and who have played a role for a great number of performances, who would claim they had succeeded with equal thoroughness in believing every action. That, however, is the aim of creative actors whether they are performing professionally, or nonprofessionally in an educational or community theatre. They work to accomplish it at every rehearsal and performance. They are extremely cautious of resorting to devices which they cannot justify in terms of the character's inner needs.

In performance a characterization usually consists of a series of actions some of which are more believable than others. Failure to achieve complete belief in every action does not indicate a bad actor any more than failure to return every ball indicates a bad tennis player. A good actor succeeds in believing a large proportion of the action, just as a good tennis player succeeds in returning a large proportion of the balls. Both the actor and the tennis player work constantly to improve their technique in order to increase the proportion of their successes.

In summary, the steps by which an actor develops a character may be listed as

1) analyze the role to discover the character's motivating desire;

2) state the desire in the form of a specific wish which will stimulate definite action;

3) explore your "inner resources" to discover what you would do to satisfy this basic desire;

4) reconcile what you would do with what the character does in the play;

5) choose one small action in the role in which you can readily believe;

6) relate this action to the motivating desire;

7) supply imaginary circumstances to complete the information given by the dramatist;

8) select externals which will help you to believe the character in this situation;

9) rehearse the action until you can believably repeat it at will;

10) break the entire role into small units of action;

11) extend this process of inducing belief to each action in the role.

EXERCISE: You are now ready to try your wings in developing a character from a play. Let us hope you will have the opportunity to develop a character subtle enough to make the problem interesting, but not complex enough to make it discouraging. Let us hope you will have the advantage of developing a character that is essentially true—not one in which the dramatist has attempted literal representation of life necessarily, but one in which he has made a truthful observation of life. Melodramatic and falsely romantic characters are unusually demanding upon the actor's powers of believing. Finally, let us hope you will have the privilege of associating with a group who share your ideals and are willing to work as hard as you are.

CHAPTER 9

Getting into the Play

The creation of character is the actor's most important contribution to the art of the theatre and his greatest responsibility as a creative artist. But when we look at the entire picture, we see that a single character is only a part of a much larger whole. This larger whole is, of course, the complete production in which all the elements of theatre art are involved. The actor must find how the character he is creating is related both to the play as a whole and to the production which the director has designed as a means of expressing the play to an audience. He must learn his proper relationship to the other characters as well as to all the elements of modern production, including lights, scenery, costumes, music, and many more. He must learn to fulfill his function in an extremely demanding group enterprise. The process of producing a play is a truly fine example of cooperative effort—a process described by Harold Clurman as "the relating of a number of talents to a single meaning." [1] Finding this *single meaning* is the responsibility of everyone involved in the production. And this meaning may be found in no other way than in discovering the author's basic purpose as it is revealed in the play itself.

Chapter 7 of this book discussed the concept of "the actor in the part" in which we learned that the actor must analyze a character with considerable care to determine the *motivating force* behind his actions. In this present chapter we shall discover that a dramatist employs a group of characters, all motivated by different and often conflicting desires, for the purpose of expressing some single or total meaning. Further, we shall be concerned with how the actor employs his individual role as an aid in realizing the author's basic intention.

Finding the Dramatist's Basic Intention

Knowing what a play is about, what "single meaning" the dramatist had in mind when he wrote it, is necessary if the actor is to fulfill his function in the cooperative effort of a dramatic production. Stanislavski wrote about this necessity: "The main theme must be firmly fixed in the actor's mind throughout the performance. It gave birth to the writing of

---

[1] Harold Clurman, *The Fervent Years: The Story of the Group Theatre and the Thirties* (New York: Alfred A. Knopf, Inc., 1945), p. 41.

the play. It should also be the fountain-head of the actor's artistic creation." [2] He frequently referred to this main theme as the *super-objective.*

In a play the whole stream of individual, minor objectives, all the imaginative thoughts, feelings, and actions of an actor, should converge to carry out the super-objective *of the plot. The common bond must be so strong that even the most insignificant detail, if it is not related to the* super-objective, *will stand out as superfluous or wrong.* [3]

Following Stanislavski, Harold Clurman states emphatically that "no character of the play can be properly understood unless the play as a whole is understood." He recognizes that understanding the play as a whole resolves itself into one question:

What is the basic action of the play? *What is the play about from the standpoint of the characters' principal conflict? . . . What is the play's core? For Gordon Craig,* Hamlet *is the story of a man's search for truth. Saroyan's* My Heart's in the Highlands, *to its New York director, was the story of people eager to give things to one another—lovers all, in a sense. For me, Odets'* Night Music *had to do with the search for a home.*

Whether these formulations are correct or not, the point is that the director's most important task is to find the basic line of the play. I call it the spine *of the play because my first teacher in this field, Richard Boleslavsky, used the word.* [4]

Finding the dramatist's basic intention may well be considered the "director's most important task," and one of his most important responsibilities is teaching the basic intention of the play to his cast of actors. But the actor, if he is to be a creative artist in his own right, needs to understand the meaning of the play as a whole through his own efforts. Only then will he be able to make it the primary source of his characterization. How does the actor discover this basic meaning?

In *The Proposal* we found Lomov's motivating desire to be "I want to destroy anything that challenges my ego." We decided that Natalya's actions are motivated by the same basic wish, and that the conflict of

---

[2] Constantin Stanislavski, *An Actor Prepares* (New York: Theatre Arts Books, 1936), p. 258. Copyright, 1936, by Theatre Arts, Inc. Reprinted by permission of the publisher, Theatre Arts Books, 224 West 4th Street, New York 14, New York.

[3] *Ibid.,* p. 256.

[4] Harold Clurman, "The Principles of Interpretation," in John Gassner, ed., *Producing the Play* (New York: The Dryden Press, 1941), p. 285. Copyright, 1941. Reprinted by special permission of John Gassner and The Dryden Press.

the play results from bringing two such people together. To understand Chekhov's basic intention, what it was that "gave birth" to this particular play, we must determine what the play is about from the standpoint of this conflict.

In attempting to find the meaning of the play as a whole, we must recognize at the very beginning that we shall not be able to determine the dramatist's intention solely from an examination of the plot or story. The plot is rarely the unique feature of a dramatic work. Essentially the same story may be used, in fact, to express a variety of meanings. To find the real significance we must look below the surface to see how the dramatist has used his plot to express some observation about human behavior. People who are interested only in "the story" of a play are missing a good deal of its value. And a play which offers nothing but "a story" is realizing only a small part of its possibilities.

The story of *The Proposal* may be told in three short sentences. Two people quarrel. They become engaged. They continue quarreling.

Immediately we recognize the importance of a second dramatic element—character. These are not just any two people. They are Lomov with his ego and his nerves and his ridiculous evening clothes, and Natalya with her ego and her efficiency and her apron. So in addition to telling the story, the action of the plot serves to reveal these two interesting persons.

Both plot and character serve to express a third essential element of the dramatic structure. This element is generally called the *theme*. It is the observation on life which was the dramatist's basic purpose in writing the play. Revealing this observation to the audience is the actor's basic purpose when the play is produced upon the stage.

What is the theme of *The Proposal?* The play surely cannot be merely a story of two people quarreling. To fill the stage with a noisy wrangle has little point unless the quarrel is directed toward some further end. If the play is only the story of two people's becoming engaged, it certainly is like half of all the other plays ever written. What purpose do the quarrel and the engagement serve? The fact that there is considerable humor in the two people's interrupting a quarrel only long enough to become engaged does not make it unnecessary for us to determine Chekhov's theme. The writer of comedy makes an observation about life that is just as true, and often just as serious, as the writer of other types of drama. And the production of a comedy has significance in proportion to the extent that the actors are able to make that observation clear to the audience.

In answering the question as to what observation Chekhov was making in this story of the quarrel and the engagement, we must give attention to two points in the play:

1) Both quarrels are over entirely *trivial* matters.

2) To both Lomov and Natalya becoming engaged is a *serious* matter. They both indicate that they seriously want to become engaged.

The play, then, must be about people who make trivial matters more important than serious matters.

In trying to state the theme more clearly, we logically ask *why* these people argue so violently about such petty things. We know, of course, they do it because they are both self-centered egotists. So perhaps we may say that the play is about people who sacrifice important concerns by asserting their egos in trivial ways. Such a theme augments and gives direction to the characters as we have discovered them. Furthermore, it may be easily reconciled with a basic theme in nearly all of Chekhov's work—the triviality of the lives of the Russian *bourgeoisie*.

Here then is the basic idea or the theme as it might be stated by a reader or a critic, and as it would be comprehended by an audience seeing a production of the play.

The actors (and the director) need to go still further by determining how the dramatist has made his theme clear through a consolidated action that constitutes the dramatic conflict. The action which embodies the theme is what Stanislavski calls the *super-objective* and what Harold Clurman refers to as the *spine* of the play. It serves as a constant guide to the director and the actors because it is the principal unifying factor for all details of the performance. We may say that the spine of *The Proposal* is "to stand up for one's rights."

It may help to illustrate further by determining the theme and the super-objective of *Romeo and Juliet*. The theme of Shakespeare's play might be stated as "the triumph of love over hatred." In the final scene (the scene in which it is usual for the dramatist to reveal most fully his observation about life) we find that because of the great love between Romeo and Juliet the "canker'd hate" between the Montagues and the Capulets is finally ended. The ancient rivalry will exist no more. The two families at last will live together, without rancor, in peace and harmony.

The spine of *Romeo and Juliet* may be stated as "to overcome all obstacles in the path of love." This is the consolidated action which

embodies the theme. It is the super-objective which guides the actors and
the director throughout the production.

There is sometimes a mistaken notion on the part of beginning
actors that careful analysis destroys spontaneity in a performance. This
attitude is difficult to defend. In the first place, acting, like any other
art, is a highly conscious process. It is not actually spontaneous; it only
appears to be so. Secondly, spontaneity which is not directed toward
some single purpose is of little or no value on the stage.

The beginning actor's resistance to thorough study of the play
as a whole may be especially strong in the case of a comedy, where he
assumes the play has no purpose other than to be comical. Actually,
although some plays are based upon a theme that is essentially comic in
itself in its reversal of some generally accepted standard of behavior,
the dramatist's basic intention may be no different in comedy than in
the so-called serious types of drama. The difference lies in his treatment
of the theme. For the actor the difference is not a matter of whether or
not to analyze the play; knowing the meaning of the play as a whole is
essential in any case. The difference for the actor, as he goes from one
type of play to another, is primarily a matter of the attitude he assumes
toward the character he is playing.

It is the actor's attitude toward the character and toward the play as
a whole to which we now turn our attention.

Interpreting the Play:
The Dual Personality of the Actor

In discharging his responsibility as an instrument in communicating the
meaning of the play to an audience, the actor assumes a dual personality.
Figuratively, he splits himself into two parts. One part is the actor in
the character. Up to now we have been primarily concerned with that
aspect of the actor's problem. The other part of the actor remains outside of the character as a *commentator* continually pointing out to the
audience the significance, in relation to the total meaning of the play,
of what the character is doing and saying.

It is a truism in the theatre that the actor must not "lose himself in
his part." The most frequently quoted statement of this obvious truth
is George Bernard Shaw's maxim: "The one thing not forgivable in an
actor is *being* the part instead of *playing* it." In these warnings against
losing oneself in the part and against being the character instead of play-

ing it are a recognition of the necessity of the actor's divided personality.

The dramatist has not written character sketches merely for the purpose of acquainting an audience with a particular group of people. He has drawn his characters in order to make some observation about life which he believes to be true. So the actor's twofold function is

1) to create the character, and

2) to use his creation as a means of expressing the dramatist's observation.

In other words, in addition to creating the character and bringing him into existence upon the stage, the actor must *comment* upon his creation to the extent of telling the audience what the dramatist, and very possibly what he himself, thinks of the character's behavior.

Once again *The Proposal* will serve as illustration. In playing Lomov, the actor devotes a part of himself to creating a character in which he and the audience can believe. The other part is devoted to telling the audience that Lomov is an absurd egotist. The "comment" upon the character must point out that Lomov's evening clothes are ridiculous; that his violent quarreling is petty and pointless; that his concern about his health is only a bid for attention that he may feel more self-important. In playing Natalya, the actress expresses a similar pettiness in her behavior which is perhaps even more ridiculous than Lomov's. Having the ability to manage her father's farm, she might well be expected to refrain from such a display of egotism. Together the actors of these two parts suggest to the audience the inevitable outcome of the proposal. The "married bliss" is certain to be marred, indeed we might say permanently scarred, by the frequent occurrences of such violent upheavals.

In making his comment, the actor guides the audience in forming an opinion of the character and, thus, leads them to an understanding of the basic meaning of the play. The comment may say, for instance, that a certain character is weak but essentially good; that although it may not be possible to approve all his actions, he is entitled at least to sympathetic understanding. It may say that another character is vain and selfish, almost completely undeserving of sympathy. It may say still another is living fully and happily according to an eminently sound set of principles.

It is of great importance in realizing the total meaning of any play that the actor's comments express the dramatist's intention, as nearly as it is possible to discover what that intention is. To make the audience dislike a character whom the playwright intended to be received with sympathy would almost certainly alter the essential values of the play. Obviously it would be very wrong to interpret *Romeo and Juliet* in such a way that the long-standing feud between the Montagues and the Capulets seemed justified and the love between the two young people seemed like a flagrant breach of family loyalty.

Proportioning the Parts

In the matter of the *dual personality*, then, the actor must decide what the "comment" on a character should be in order best to express the meaning of the play as a whole. He also has the further problem of determining what proportion of his total personality is to be *character* and, consequently, what proportion is to be *commentator*. A decision in this matter will be based largely on the type of play the dramatist has written and the style of production the director has planned.

We frequently see references to different styles of acting. There is no doubt that they exist. The actor may be called upon to play a number of characters in a wide variety of styles. The differences are occasioned by

1) the historical period in which the play was written (a classic Greek play is not acted like a modern play),

2) the type of play (a farce is not acted like a tragedy),

3) the style of the play and/or the production (a naturalistic play is not acted like a romantic play).

It is not in order here to consider the differences between comedy and tragedy or between realism and expressionism. Such a consideration would in itself be a fit subject for another book. Such books, in fact, have been written, and the thoughtful actor will want to become acquainted with them. But since a beginning actor (especially in college or university) is as likely to be confronted with Elizabethan tragedy as with modern realistic comedy, it is in order here to relate our basic approach toward the entire problem of acting to the demands of these different styles.

We may say at the outset that the basic approach is essentially the same for all periods, types, and styles. The differences, insofar as the actor is concerned, lie in the *extent* to which he "comments" upon the character and the *manner* in which the comment is made. The problem imposed by differences of type and style is fundamentally a matter of finding the proper proportion between that part of the actor which is the character and that part which is the commentator upon the character.

We may illustrate briefly. Comedy may be described as "a way of looking at life with the mind rather than with the passions," asking of an audience "detached observation rather than emotional involvement." [5] It follows that tragedy is primarily emotional, rather than intellectual, looking at life "not only seriously but in a mood of exalted fascination." It is sometimes said that the effect of tragedy is that man is noble, whereas the effect of comedy is that man is ridiculous. In between these two general types is a third genre called, for want of a better name, *serious drama*. Although many dramas of this type leave us with a feeling that life is futile, the attitude of the playwright may be more objective. He may find man neither noble nor ridiculous and he may want to leave the audience with mixed feelings about his characters.

In comedy the audience remains more emotionally detached than in tragedy or serious drama; we do not find it easy to laugh at a person for whom we have emotional sympathy. This being true, the actor of comedy best serves his function by remaining somewhat detached from the role. He creates a believable character; then he figuratively holds the character up to the audience for them to ridicule and enjoy, some feeling of superiority being necessary to the comic response. In fact, the actor himself enjoys the ridiculousness of the character he is playing, and he has a keen sense of sharing his enjoyment with the audience. In comedy, then, the proportion of the actor which serves as *commentator* is greater than in tragedy or in serious drama. In these latter types the desirable response from the audience is emotional involvement, a sympathy or antipathy toward the characters, and, in tragedy at least, identification with the character of the hero. In these types the actor himself becomes more emotionally involved, and the proportion of the actor as commentator is consequently decreased.

To illustrate briefly what is meant by *styles of theatre,* a distinction not identical with the types of drama mentioned above, we may recognize two basic approaches for either the dramatist or the director. In approaching a play *realistically,* the dramatist or director or actor desires to create on the stage a representation of life that will *appear* to be actual or real. The scenery looks like a real room. The costumes look like real

---

[5] For a concise account of types and styles of drama see John Gassner, *Producing the Play* (New York: The Dryden Press, 1941), pp. 44–93.

clothes. The actors look like real people. Any arrangement or heightening of details for the purpose of pointing the meaning of the play must be accomplished in such a way that the illusion of reality for the audience is not destroyed. In a *nonrealistic* approach illusion of reality may be sacrificed to arrangement and exaggeration of detail in order to make the significance of the play more obvious.

In a production of *Romeo and Juliet,* for example, the director might decide that yellow-green was the proper color to symbolize Romeo's lovesickness in the opening scenes. In approaching the play realistically, he would probably have Romeo in a costume which was predominately yellow-green, and it would have to look like proper attire for the Italian Renaissance. In approaching the play nonrealistically, the director might without regard for country or period require a yellow-green costume that expressed the essential quality of Romeo's state of mind. And he might, if he were an extremist, make up Romeo's face and hands a yellow-green to emphasize the lovesickness from which he suffers. Similarly, instead of having Tybalt merely move with a kind of feline grace and stealth, he might have him made up actually to look like a cat and possibly make catlike noises when his anger is aroused. In the nonrealistic production costumes, make-up, movement, gesture, facial expression, voice quality, intonation, all may be exaggerated for the purpose of pointing up the meanings of the play.

Making Contact with the Audience

It is in order to mention one other problem the actor faces in adjusting his basic method to the varying demands of different types of plays. This is the matter of the degree to which the actor appears to be aware of the presence of the audience. Our modern theatre, for the most part, is a realistic or illusionistic theatre. It is based on the tradition of the "fourth wall" through which the audience sees the actors, but through which the actor must not *appear* to see the audience. The impression which many modern plays aim to produce is that there on the stage is a piece of action which the audience has the privilege of observing, but which would go on in the same way whether or not they were there. This concept of theatre is sometimes called *representational* because the actor is attempting to represent before the audience action as it happens in life. He makes no direct contact with his observers because to do so would destroy the illusion. Any adjustments he makes to the presence of the audience (such as always speaking in a voice loud enough to be heard, holding his lines for the laughs, and taking pains to perform all action so that everyone may see it) must appear "natural" or lifelike; they must be clearly motivated in terms of the desire of the character he is playing.

In earlier periods, and in some few modern plays, the approach is *presentational* or nonillusionistic. Instead of trying to represent events on the stage as they would happen in life, the actor frankly accepts the contrived circumstances under which the plays are given. He *presents* the play directly to the audience without attempting to conceal the theatrical devices he is using.

The ultimate in presentationalism is the traditional Chinese theatre. The Chinese recognize frankly that the conditions of the theatre are not real. Consequently, they do not find any necessity for creating an illusion of reality. On their stage they will readily accept an actor astride a pole as a general on horseback. The property man sits at the side of the stage in full view of the audience and provides the actors with hand "props" as they need them. The magic of their theatre comes from the formal manner in which they present truthful observation of life without attempting to represent life upon the stage. They distinguish to a much greater extent than we the difference between *truth* and *actuality*.

In some respects the classic plays—the plays of Sophocles and Shakespeare and Sheridan and Molière—are closer to the Chinese theatre than to our modern illusionistic stage. They are *presentational* in that they do not attempt to represent life in a realistic environment. They are not as frankly theatrical as the Chinese plays with their visible property men, but they do permit the actor a much greater frankness in recognizing the presence of the audience. In the soliloquies he may tell the character's thoughts directly to the audience, and in the "asides" he may comment directly to them upon the action of the play.

Summary

In these general distinctions of different types and styles there is some suggestion of necessary differences in acting. More important than the differences, however, is the fact that in every case the basic approach is the same. No matter what type or style of drama he may be concerned with, the actor begins his preparation by discovering what is essentially true in the role he has been called upon to play. He continues by embodying that truth in a character in which he and the audience can believe. He brings his creation into existence by a series of actions through which the character attempts to satisfy some fundamental desire.

In addition to bringing the character into existence, the actor uses his role as an instrument in expressing the total meaning of the play. To fulfill this function he emphasizes those aspects of the character which point up this meaning—Romeo's lovesickness, Tybalt's viciousness, the Nurse's bawdiness, Lomov's ego. This emphasis of certain character traits is what we have been referring to as "commenting" upon the character. Sometimes, as in the case of realistic serious drama, the comment is very subtle; the audience is never consciously aware that it is being made. Sometimes, as in the case of farce or a nonrealistic production, the comment may be very obvious. Always it serves to make some truth about the character clear to the audience, and always it must be kept in its proper proportion. That proportion is determined by the basic style in which the play is being produced.

EXERCISE: a) At the end of Chapter 7, to help in the problem of finding the motivating desire of an individual character, you were asked to choose a major role from a standard play for detailed study. Return now to this same play for the purpose of determining the *theme* which you think was the unifying factor in the dramatist's mind. State the theme briefly and clearly.

b) Now determine the *super-objective* from a study of the extended dramatic action which embodies the theme. State it clearly in terms which stimulate each actor to action and which, at the same time, will make clear how each character is related to the basic idea which you discovered to be the theme of the play. (Remember when a group is working together upon the production of a play, general agreement about the theme and the super-objective is necessary. Obviously no unity would be possible if each actor were working toward a different purpose. The most desirable means of arriving at a general agreement is through group discussion under the guidance of the director, each actor having prepared for the discussion by an independent analysis.)

c) List the character traits upon which you want to "comment" in your performance in order to point up the total meaning of the play.

d) Describe the *manner* in which you will make the comment in order to harmonize your style of acting with the demands of the play and the production.

EXERCISE: Read a number of plays in order to increase your understanding of the different types and styles of drama. Here is a suggested list for a beginning.

Lillian Hellman: *The Little Foxes*
Eugene O'Neill: *Beyond the Horizon*
Henrik Ibsen: *A Doll's House*
Arthur Miller: *Death of a Salesman* and *The Crucible*
Elmer Rice: *The Adding Machine*
Kaufman and Connelly: *Beggar on Horseback*
Sheridan: *The Rivals*
Goldsmith: *She Stoops to Conquer*
Shakespeare: *Hamlet* and *The Taming of the Shrew*
Euripides: *Alcestis*
Sophocles: *Antigone*

As you read these plays, answer the following questions in regard to them:

1) What truthful observation about life has the dramatist made which underlies the play as a whole?

2) To what extent are the characters realistic; that is, to what extent do they speak and behave like people in actual life?

3) To what extent are they not realistic; that is, what means which are not consistent with lifelike behavior has the dramatist used to express his observations? (An additional illustration may help you to answer this question. When Macbeth hears of the death of his wife, he expresses his feelings in a magnificent speech beginning

> Tomorrow and tomorrow and tomorrow
> Creeps in its petty pace from day to day.

He speaks *unrealistically* because in actual life no one is able to express his feelings with such effect. Certainly, however, he speaks *truthfully* because his words express the very essence of disillusionment and self-realization.)

4) Imagine yourself faced with the problem of acting various roles from these plays. What are some of the things you would have to do that you consider realistic—things that would help you and the audience to believe in the existence of the character?

5) What are some of the things you would have to do that you consider unrealistic—things the dramatist has planned to express to the audience the significance of his observations?

CHAPTER 10

Interpreting the Lines

So far we have mentioned only in passing the problem of interpreting the lines. This problem is, of course, a matter of considerable importance. In spite of the truth of such old adages as "Seeing is believing" and "Actions speak louder than words," one of the actor's prime responsibilities is to communicate the meaning of the dramatist's lines to the audience.

The basis for effective interpretation of lines is a good voice. It would be possible to quote a number of very great actors to the effect that the voice is the most important of the actor's attributes. Again let us recognize that trying to estimate the relative importance of the various essentials of acting is like trying to determine which of the four wheels is more vital to the automobile. Certainly an actor must speak. Certainly it is true that to the extent his voice is not as good as it could be, to that extent is he a less effective actor than he could be. His voice and his body are the instruments through which an actor reaches his audience. He will want to have them trained so that he has the finest possible instruments at his command.

Anyone interested in achieving success in acting at any level will seek instruction in how to improve his voice, and he will regularly practice systematic exercises in diction and voice production. Assuming the absence of physiological defects which can be corrected only by surgery, there is no voice so poor that it will not respond to proper training; and there is no voice so fine that it could not be better if it were given the advantage of proper exercise. In training his voice, the actor should seek to accomplish several objectives. He should seek to acquire

1) *volume*, so that his voice may be heard without difficulty;

2) *relaxation*, so that his voice will not tire unduly during a long performance and so that he will not involuntarily raise his pitch during moments of tension and emotional strain;

3) *quality* which is pleasant to hear and capable of expressing varying emotional states; quality is to a large extent a matter of resonance;

4) *articulation*, so that he may be readily understood even in passages requiring deft and rapid speech;

5) *pronunciation* which is free from slovenliness and provincial influences;

6) *flexibility*, so that his voice is capable of considerable variety of volume, quality, and pitch; the best voice for the stage is the voice that can do the most things with the greatest ease;

7) *ability to hear* the voice and to recognize subtle variations in pitch and quality; ear training is as important for the actor as for the musician.

Although the voice responds readily to proper exercises and it is usually possible to notice improvement after a few weeks of practice, the accomplishment of these objectives entails an extensive period of training. It is conservative to say that a normal voice requires at least two years of daily exercise before it is capable of meeting the demands imposed upon an actor who is attempting a variety of roles. This is basic training which no beginning actor can afford to forego.

Probably in no particular are American actors as a class less effective than in the use of their voices. Nonprofessional actors, of considerable ability and technical skill otherwise, are often quite inadequate vocally. Their voices lack the authority necessary to command attention. They cannot make themselves heard with ease. Their pitch is unpleasantly high in scenes of emotional excitement. Their articulation and pronunciation do not insure the greatest clarity in communicating the meaning of the lines.

Such shortcomings, however, are by no means confined to the nonprofessional stage. One of the commonest complaints of audiences in New York is not being able to hear the lines. Many actors who have been successful in modern plays find their voices woefully deficient when they attempt the classics. These vocal inadequacies are amazing considering the high standards of production that otherwise prevail in the professional theatre. No one laments the passing of the rhetorical style of acting which was so highly admired during the nineteenth century. But there is no gain without some loss. From all accounts the "old style" players could be heard and understood without difficulty.

The actor must consciously train his voice so that in performance he can use it subconsciously as an instrument for expressing the thoughts and emotions of the character he is playing. The fact that a procedure for such training is not described here is in no way intended to minimize its importance. The training of the actor's voice as an effective instrument should be directed by the most competent teacher of voice and diction available. Here we are concerned with *what* he expresses rather than with the training of the actor as an instrument.

From what has gone before, it is not difficult to understand that a character in a play *speaks* for the same reason that he *acts*—to aid in the satisfaction of some basic desire. The question always in the actor's mind, then, as he seeks to interpret his lines is "*Why* does the character say what he says at this particular moment?"

Finding the Under-Meaning of the Lines

Finding the meaning of the lines is always a matter of discovering what the character *wants to result* from what he is saying. It is always a matter of finding the motivation beneath the speeches. In seeking this motivation the actor must consider

1) how a line relates to the fundamental desire which he has decided is the motivating force behind all of the character's actions,

2) how a line relates to its immediate context, especially to the line that has just preceded it.

A line which cannot in some way be made to serve the character in accomplishing his basic purpose will be one of those details which Stanislavski said will stand out in the production as "superfluous or wrong." A line which cannot be related to its immediate context will baffle both the actor and the audience because it will seem pointless and illogical.

In determining these relations, it is of considerable importance to understand that the real significance of a line rarely lies in the meaning of the words themselves or in the literal information which the words convey. A line rarely serves solely to give information. It has more to express than its mere surface meaning. Such a simple bit of dialogue as

BOB. What time is it?
ANN. It is eleven o'clock.

has no dramatic significance until the meaning beneath the lines is known. Why does one character ask the time in the first place? What is in the other character's mind when she answers the question?

It is obvious that these words can convey a number of different meanings depending upon the circumstances under which they are spoken, which is another way of saying, depending upon the context which surrounds them. In a melodramatic play, Bob might be in the death cell awaiting execution, and the lines might mean

BOB. How much longer do I have to live?
ANN. Exactly an hour. You are to be executed at midnight.

In another play the speakers might be listening to a dull and seemingly endless lecture, and the lines might mean

BOB. When is this thing going to end?
ANN. The bell will ring in about thirty seconds.

Again, the situation might be one in which the speakers were engaged in some engrossing activity, and the meaning might be

BOB. We've completely lost track of the time.
ANN. We're late already for our appointment with Mr. Higgins.

It is of the greatest importance here to recognize that to find the under-meaning of a line is not to paraphrase it, or merely to restate the words of the author in the words of the actor. Paraphrasing, indeed, may be necessary to understanding lines when their surface meaning is not immediately clear; the actor may find it especially worth while to restate in his own words all the lines of a verse play. But after the paraphrase, he *still* has the problem of finding what is beneath the line, how it is related to the dramatic action and to the motivating desire of the character. To find the under-meaning we must consider the *action-impulse* inherent in the line. Hamlet's famous "To be or not to be," for example, may be paraphrased very simply as "To live or not to live." The *action-impulse* beneath the line is to decide whether or not to kill himself.

When Bob asks "What time is it?" meaning "How much longer do I have to live?" the action-impulse is to hold back the time. When he means "When is this thing going to end?" his action-impulse is to get out of a dull lecture. When he means "We have completely lost track of the time," the action inherent in the line is to break off what he and Ann are doing and get started to keep their appointment.

The significance of a line is not on the surface but beneath it. The real meaning is the under-meaning. When speaking a line, the actor does not think only of the words he is saying, but also of the action-impulse inherent in the line.

In Oscar Wilde's famous satire on snobbery, *The Importance of Being Earnest*, the haughty Lady Bracknell speaks slightingly of the family background of Cecily Cardew. Cecily's guardian, Jack Worthing, replies,

> Miss Cardew is the grand-daughter of the late Mr. Thomas Cardew of 149 Belgrave Square, S. W.; Gervase Park, Dorking, Surrey; and the Sporran, Fifeshire, N. B.

To give the addresses of the late Mr. Thomas Cardew's three residences is not Jack's purpose. The under-meaning is

> My ward is a person of excellent family connections which may be quite as acceptable in English society as your own, Lady Bracknell!

The action-impulse is to put Lady Bracknell in her place.

Earlier in the play Jack has been informed that Lady Bracknell does not quite approve of him either. He *says*, "May I ask why not?" But the line *means*, "I am sure I don't see why she doesn't approve of me. I am every bit as good as she is." Here the action-impulse is to assert his equality.

Relating the Lines to the Motivating Desire

Even after the actor has found the under-meaning and the action-impulse, he has not yet fully realized the significance of the line. He still must relate the meaning to the motivating desire of the character he is playing. He must understand how the line serves the purpose of helping the character to *get what he wants* in the play, and he must make that purpose clear to the audience.

In the situation in which Bob is in the death cell awaiting execution, for example, Bob's motivating desire must be clearly in the actor's mind before he can give the line its full value. The behavior of a character in such a circumstance might be motivated in any one of several ways. If the condemned man feels only the primal urge to live, if he is hoping for a reprieve from the governor or even hoping blindly for a miracle, his asking for the time is essentially a cry for help. If he has accepted his death as inevitable, his motivating desire might be to seek redemption for his crime, and his line might be a plea for more time in which to make atonement. Even at the point of death he might still be filled with the same bitterness which led him originally to commit the crime, and he might want more than anything else to give no one the satisfaction of seeing any sign of remorse. In this case, the line would be a declaration of his intention to refrain from making any repentance.

Ann's basic purpose must also be thoroughly understood to realize the meaning of such a simple line as, "It is eleven o'clock." If she is Bob's devoted and loyal wife, her motivating desire will be to comfort her husband. Her line will be an expression of love and faith. If, to imagine a highly melodramatic situation, Ann is a rival spy with a basic wish to coerce Bob to reveal vital information before he dies, her line might be a threat to harm members of his family if he refuses her request.

To draw a further illustration from *The Importance of Being Earnest*, Jack Worthing wants to marry Lady Bracknell's daughter. When he asks why Lady Bracknell does not approve of him, he is attempting to assert his own sense of superiority against the onslaught of this overpowering dowager with whom he may have to cope as a mother-in-law. When he tells her of Mr. Cardew's three addresses, he is attempting to equalize the score between them by returning a bit of her own brand of snobbishness.

Examination of some short passages of dialogue from *The Proposal* may provide further help in understanding the problem of relating a character's line to his motivating desire. This interchange between Lomov and Natalya is the beginning of the quarrel over the ownership of the land:

LOMOV. . . . You will remember that my Oxen Meadows touch your birchwoods.

NATALYA. Excuse my interrupting you. You say, "My Oxen Meadows . . . ." But are they yours?

LOMOV. Yes, mine.

NATALYA. What are you talking about? Oxen Meadows are ours, not yours!

LOMOV. No, mine, honoured Natalya Stepanovna.

NATALYA. Well, I never knew that before. How do you make that out?

LOMOV. How? I'm speaking of those Oxen Meadows which are wedged in between your birchwoods and the Burnt Marsh.

NATALYA. Yes, yes. . . . They're ours!

Both of these characters, we must remember, want more than anything else to preserve their own egotistical natures. Almost any subject they could choose for conversation would be sure to lead to a sharp conflict of personalities. Although just a little later Lomov presents his claim to the land at some length, during this passage he is merely putting up a dogged resistance.

Natalya is making the attack here, and there is another meaning beneath her apparent politeness when she says, "Excuse my interrupting you." Actually she is saying, "If you think I am going to let you get away with calling Oxen Meadows yours, you certainly don't know me very well."

Beneath her line, "What are you talking about?" she means, "You are talking outrageous nonsense."

When she says, "Well, I never knew that before," she is taunting Lomov by implying, "And I don't know it now either."

Later Natalya's father becomes involved, and the quarrel reaches the abusive stage. Finally Lomov takes refuge in his "ill health and delicate nerves" and runs for home.

CHUBUKOV. Your grandfather was a drunkard, and your younger aunt, Nastasya Mihailovna, ran away with an architect. . . .

LOMOV. And your mother was hump-backed. (*Clutches at his side*) Something pulling in my side. . . . My head. Help! Water!

CHUBUKOV. Your father was a guzzling gambler!

NATALYA. And there haven't been many gossips to equal your aunt.

LOMOV. My left foot has gone to sleep. . . . You're an intriguer. . . . Oh, my heart! And it's an open secret that before the last election you bri. . . . I can see stars. . . . Where's the door? Oh! . . . I think I'm dying. . . . My foot's quite numb. (*Goes to the door*)

CHUBUKOV. (*Following him*) And don't set foot in my house again.

NATALYA. Take it to court! We'll see!

LOMOV *staggers out.*

The action-impulse of each of the characters here is "to abuse his opponent." All of these lines directly serve Lomov and Natalya in satisfying their basic desire of maintaining their egos—a desire to which they are willing to sacrifice many other needs along with their personal dignity.

Relating the Lines to the Dramatist's Basic Intention

The actor must also be aware of how the lines serve to realize the dramatist's basic intention or how they aid in communicating the central idea of the play to the audience. This problem has been anticipated in such previous steps as (1) finding the character's motivating desire—a process in which the lines themselves were an important consideration, (2) relating this fundamental desire to the meaning of the play as a whole, and (3) finding the *under-meaning* and the *action-impulse* of the lines, which, as we have seen, may be accomplished only by relating the lines to other elements in the play.

Once these steps have been completed, it is likely the actor will understand how the dramatist intended each line to aid in the expression of his basic theme. We have said that the central idea of *The Proposal* has to do with people who sacrifice important things by asserting their egos in trivial ways. In relating the lines to this basic theme, it is important, then, that the pettiness of the quarrel be emphasized. No one in the audience must be in doubt that "Oxen Meadows" is a worthless piece of land. It must also be made clear that there is no real advantage to either Natalya or Lomov in settling which hunting dog is superior. At the same time, the lines must be related to the basic purpose by indicating the seriousness with which the quarrel is waged. It begins with polite restraint in such lines as

NATALYA. Excuse my interrupting you.

and

LOMOV. No, mine, honoured Natalya Stepanovna.

Both quarrelers become indignant in such lines as

NATALYA. No, you're simply joking, or making fun of me. . . . What a surprise. We've had the land for three hundred years, and then suddenly we are told that it isn't ours. I can hardly believe my own ears.

and

LOMOV. Then you make out that I'm a land-grabber? Madam, never in my life have I grabbed anybody else's land, and I shan't allow anyone to accuse me of having done so. . . .

Later, as they become positively outraged, the lines further point up the triviality of the quarrel, the seriousness of the quarrelers, and the ridiculousness of the whole situation.

LOMOV. . . . Oxen Meadows are mine!
NATALYA. It's not true, they're ours!
LOMOV. Mine!
NATALYA. It's not true! I'll prove it! I'll send my mowers out to the Meadows this very day!
LOMOV. What?
NATALYA. My mowers will be there this very day!

LOMOV. I'll give it to them in the neck!

NATALYA. You dare!

LOMOV. Oxen Meadows are mine! You understand? Mine!

NATALYA. Please don't shout! You can shout yourself hoarse in your own house, but here I must ask you to restrain yourself.

LOMOV. If it wasn't, madam, for this awful excruciating palpitation, if my whole inside wasn't upset, I'd talk to you in a different way. (*Yells*) Oxen Meadows are mine!

NATALYA. Ours!

LOMOV. Mine!

NATALYA. Ours!

LOMOV. Mine!

The Importance of Being Earnest is another play about people who are concerned with trivialities. It is a satire upon the snobbish upper classes at the close of the last century who sought to relieve their boredom by concentrating upon inconsequentials. Oscar Wilde saw the comic possibilities in the affectations of such people, and he ridiculed them good-naturedly in this farce. The plot has to do with two young ladies whose practically sole requirement for a husband is that his name be Ernest—a requirement which compels both Jack and Algernon to arrange to be rechristened.

The lines of the play must continually be made to serve Wilde's purpose of having fun at the expense of these people. The following bit of dialogue indicates Jack's boredom and the eagerness with which Algernon engages in trivial pursuits:

ALGERNON. . . . may I dine with you tonight at Willis's?

JACK. I suppose so, if you want to.

ALGERNON. Yes, but you must be serious about it. I hate people who are not serious about meals. It is so shallow of them.

And later

ALGERNON. . . . Now, my dear boy, if we want to get a good table at Willis's, we really must go and dress. Do you know it is nearly seven?

JACK. Oh! it is always nearly seven.

ALGERNON. Well, I'm hungry.

JACK. I never knew you when you weren't.

ALGERNON. What shall we do after dinner? Go to a theatre?

JACK. Oh, no! I loathe listening.

ALGERNON. Well, let's go to the Club.

JACK. Oh, no! I hate talking.

ALGERNON. Well, we might trot around to the Empire at ten?

JACK. Oh, no! I can't bear looking at things. It is so silly.

ALGERNON. Well, what shall we do?

JACK. Nothing!

ALGERNON. It is awfully hard work doing nothing. However, I don't mind hard work where there is no definite object of any kind.

Notice here the action-impulses of the two characters are in conflict. Algernon's impulse is "to get ready for dinner." Jack's impulse is "to remain inert."

Many times a dramatist makes his basic intention clearer and stronger through the use of contrasting elements. In such cases as this, the relationship of the lines of certain characters to the total meaning of the play is one of contrast to the central theme. The theme is thus pointed the more sharply, just as colors appear brighter when they are placed in contrast with other colors.

Romeo and Juliet, for instance, is a play about young people in love. We found its theme to be concerned with the triumph of young love over old and "canker'd hate." Although Romeo and Juliet both meet a tragic death, their love is triumphant. Because of it, the Montagues and the Capulets end their ancient feud, and civil brawls no longer disturb the quiet of Verona's streets. The theme of triumphant love is expressed throughout the play in Juliet's and Romeo's lines,

> My bounty is as boundless as the sea,
> My love as deep; the more I give to thee,
> The more I have, for both are infinite.

and

> O my love! my wife!
> Death, that has suck'd the honey of thy breath,
> Hath had no power yet upon thy beauty:
> Thou art not conquer'd; beauty's ensign yet
> Is crimson in thy lips and in thy cheeks,
> And death's pale flag is not advanced there.

Their love is made a thing of still greater beauty because it stands out in relief against the hatred of Old Montague and Old Capulet, the Nurse's vulgarity, Mercutio's mockery, Tybalt's malice, and Lady Capulet's coldness. The lines of these characters, therefore, are related to the central theme through contrast. It is important that actors playing these characters understand this relationship.

Mercutio's mocking lines emphasize the nature of Romeo's romantic love which ultimately rises above such jibes and cynicism. Tybalt's malicious lines put Romeo's new-found love to a test and finally bring about the duel that causes Romeo's banishment.

Lady Capulet unfeelingly rejects Juliet with

> Talk not to me, for I'll not speak a word:
> Do as thou wilt, for I have done with thee.

Throughout the play, Juliet's warmth and generosity stand out against her mother's unyielding practicality. These particular lines serve to emphasize the desperation of Juliet's predicament and compel her toward her final course of action.

Although the Nurse's character is vastly different from that of Lady Capulet, she serves a similar purpose in providing dramatic contrast. Juliet's sweetness and purity stand out against the Nurse's bawdiness. Her advice to Juliet to marry the Count of Paris for practical reasons, when she is already secretly married to the banished Romeo, is revolting to a person of Juliet's idealism:

> I think it best you married with the County.
> O, he's a lovely gentleman!
> Romeo's a dishclout to him: an eagle, madam,
> Hath not so green, so quick, so fair an eye
> As Paris hath. Beshrew my very heart,
> I think you are happy in this second match,
> For it excels your first: or if it did not,
> Your first is dead, or 'twere as good he were
> As living here and you no use of him.

In such instances as these, relating the lines to the dramatist's basic intention means making them serve their purpose of providing dramatic contrasts.

EXERCISE: Study carefully the lines of the character on which you are working. For each line determine

a) its *under-meaning,*

b) its *action-impulse,*

c) its relationship to the character's motivating desire (that is, what the character *wants as a result* of having said the line, and how the satisfaction of this immediate want would help him in realizing his basic motivating desire),

d) its relationship to the dramatist's basic intention or the total meaning of the play as a whole.

For the beginning actor it is excellent practice to *write out* this information.

EXERCISE: Choose a play from the list at the end of Chapter 9 and make a similar study of the lines of one or more of the characters.

Believing the Character's Manner of Speaking

The lines of a play are composed of two elements both of which are vitally important to the actor:

1) The content—what the lines say including both the surface and the under-meanings.

2) The form—the manner in which the content is expressed.

We have spent some time considering how the actor finds the *content* of the lines. We shall now consider the problem of believing the *manner* in which the character speaks.

The same meaning may be expressed in a variety of manners:

I hope it ain't gointa rain this mornin' an' spoil the picnic we was plannin' fer so long.

I trust inclement weather will not mar the outing we have been anticipating for such a time.

These two lines are essentially alike in content. The surface meanings are practically identical. The under-meanings could be exactly the same, and both lines could bear the same relation to the speaker's motivating desire. Neither is expressed in a manner which the average actor will find "natural" to his own way of speaking.

The actor's problem is to understand the background of the character's speech so that he can *believe* the manner of speaking in the same way that he believes in the character's actions. For our purposes, we shall say that the manner of speaking includes vocabulary, grammar, pronunciation, and articulation.

For the most part, these are imposed by the dramatist. The actor must accept the vocabulary that the playwright provides. The same is substantially true of the grammar. Occasionally the actor may introduce variations in pronunciation and articulation which the dramatist has not indicated, such as playing a character with a particular dialect, or with a stammer, or with "baby talk." Such variations may serve to externalize certain inner traits and help both the actor and the audience in believing them. "Baby talk," for instance, might be helpful in characterizing a young woman who as a child had been pampered and overprotected by her parents and whose motivating desire as an adult is to get the same kind of attention from her husband. Such variations, however, are justified only if they serve the actor in realizing the intentions of the dramatist.

In attempting to understand a speech background, the actor is concerned with finding circumstances given by the dramatist which justify the character's manner of speaking. In addition, as in justifying the character's actions, it is usually necessary for the actor to supply "imaginary circumstances" which, being truthful to the playwright's conception, provide a more thorough knowledge of the character (see Chapter 5).

If the manner of speaking is similar to the actor's own, or if he has frequently heard others speak in a similar way, he will have little difficulty. For example, the speech background of Joe Bonaparte and Lorna Moon in *Golden Boy*, by Clifford Odets, is so immediately comprehensible that it presents no problem to an American actor. The following bit of dialogue is typical. Lorna is trying to persuade Joe to give up his interest in the violin and become a professional prizefighter.

LORNA. . . . Joe, listen: be a fighter! Show the world! If you made your fame and fortune—and you can—you'd be anything you want. Do it! Bang your way to the lightweight crown. Get a bank account. Hire a great doctor with a beard—get your eyes fixed—

JOE. What's the matter with my eyes?

LORNA. Excuse me, I stand corrected. (*After a pause*) You get mad all the time.

JOE. That's from thinking about myself.

LORNA. How old are you Joe?

JOE. Twenty-one and a half, and the months are going fast.

LORNA. You're very smart for twenty-one and a half "and the months are going very fast."

JOE. Why not? I read every page of the Encyclopaedia Britannica. My father's friend, Mr. Carp, has it. A shrimp with glasses has to do something.[1]

In John Steinbeck's *Of Mice and Men* the speech of most of the characters presents the actors with a problem. George and Candy are hired hands on a large farm in southern California.

GEORGE. (. . . *steps to the front door, and looks out*) Say, what you doin', listenin'?

CANDY. (*Comes slowly into the room . . .*) Naw . . . I wasn't listenin'. . . . I was just standin' in the shade a minute, scratchin' my dog. I jest now finished swamping out the washhouse.

GEORGE. You was pokin' your big nose into our business! I don't like nosey guys.

CANDY. (*Looks uneasily from* GEORGE *to* LENNIE *and then back*) I jest come there . . . I didn't hear nothing you guys was sayin'. I ain't interested in nothing you was sayin'. A guy on a ranch don't never listen. Nor he don't ast no questions.

GEORGE. . . . Not if the guy wants to stay workin' long. . . .[2]

The problem in *Of Mice and Men* for the average actor is one of believing the manner of speaking in terms of his own experience. The actor may have no doubt that the speech is right and true for the character. He may understand well enough the background of lack of educational opportunities which has produced this kind of semi-illiteracy. His difficulty arises from an awareness that his own speech in a similar situation would be quite different, and such a difference is not always easy to reconcile.

Beginning efforts toward believing a variation from the actor's normal speech must often be largely mechanical or imitative. The actor may listen to himself as he forms the sounds in accordance with the dramatist's attempt to represent the character's speech upon the printed page. Some playwrights are very skillful in their use of phonetic spellings to indicate speech variations. George Bernard Shaw, for instance, was particularly adept in representing Cockney English in this way.

---

[1] Clifford Odets, *Golden Boy* (New York: Random House, Inc., 1937). Copyright, 1937, by Clifford Odets. Reprinted by permission of the publishers, Random House, Inc.

[2] John Steinbeck, *Of Mice and Men* (New York: The Viking Press, Inc., 1937). Reprinted by permission of The Viking Press, Inc.

The actor may also listen to recordings or imitate actual models if he is fortunate enough to know someone whose speech background is similar to that of the character he is playing.

If this external approach is to serve its purpose, however, it must ultimately lead the actor to believe the character's speech. And believing the speech should, in turn, increase his belief in the character as a whole. In other words, as the actor becomes convinced he has developed a manner of speaking which is true to the character, he will have a greater conviction in his total characterization.

Joe and Lorna and Candy are modest folk who use their meager speaking abilities to express their thoughts and feelings as best they can. In such a play as *The Importance of Being Earnest* we meet people with quite a different speech background. Algernon Moncrieff is, by his own admission, "immensely overeducated." He speaks not only to express his ideas, but also to impress his hearers with his cleverness and with his aptness of phrasing. All of the characters exhibit a kind of "speech embroidery" indicative of their elegance and earnest artificiality. The following lines of Gwendolen Fairfax are an example. She is talking to Cecily Cardew whom she has just learned is Jack Worthing's ward. Gwendolen and Jack have recently become engaged.

GWENDOLEN. Oh! It is strange he never mentioned to me that he had a ward. How secretive of him! He grows more interesting hourly. I am not sure, however, that the news inspires me with feelings of unmixed delight. (*Rising and going to her*) I am very fond of you, Cecily; I have liked you ever since I met you. But I am bound to state that now that I know that you are Mr. Worthing's ward, I cannot help expressing a wish you were—well, just a little older than you seem to be—and not quite so very alluring in appearance. In fact, if I may speak candidly—

CECILY. Pray do! I think that whenever one has anything unpleasant to say, one should always be quite candid.

GWENDOLEN. Well, to speak with perfect candour, Cecily, I wish that you were fully forty-two, and more than usually plain for your age. Ernest has a strong upright nature. He is the very soul of truth and honor. Disloyalty would be as impossible to him as deception. But even men of the noblest possible moral character are extremely susceptible to the influence of the physical charms of others. Modern, no less than Ancient History, supplies us with many most painful examples of what I refer to. If it were not so, indeed, History would be quite unreadable.

Such speech is the result of a background of ostentation and snobbery which is evident both in the vocabulary and in the sentence structure. Understanding of such a background is necessary if the actors are
to believe the speech and actions of the characters, and if they are to
make an adequate "comment" upon their ridiculousness.

Believing a character's manner of speaking, then, is a matter of
understanding the influences in his background that have determined his
way of speech. It is a matter of *justifying* the character's speech in terms
of his background. It is a matter of finding specific answers to such questions as

Why does one character have such an extensive vocabulary whereas
another speaks almost entirely in words of one syllable?

Why does one character speak in long involved sentences whereas
another speaks in halting fragments?

Why does one character speak with faultlessly correct grammar
whereas another says "he don't" and "we was"?

Why does one character say "you gentlemen" whereas another says
"you guys"?

Why does a character say "jist" and "git" and "goin' "?

Why does a character say "poosh" for push and "haouse" for house?

EXERCISE: a) Make a careful study of the speech of the character on which you are working. *Justify* his manner of speaking in
terms of his background. Continue your study until there is no detail
of the speech that does not seem right and true.

b) From another play choose at least one character whose manner of speaking shows a variation from your own. Make a careful
study of the speech of this character. Practice the lines until you
believe you are truthfully reproducing the character's manner of
speaking. If possible make use of actual models, phonograph records
or phonetic transcriptions.

Motivating the Longer Speech *break up*

Throughout this discussion of line interpretation we have been especially concerned with the problem of *motivation*—with relating the lines
to the character's basic desire and with making each line clearly serve a
purpose in helping the character to get what he wants. Long speeches
frequently appear difficult to the actor and frequently fail to serve their

purpose because not enough time is given to breaking the speeches into small parts, finding the under-meaning of each separate part, and relating the meaning to the character's motivating desire. The tendency of the beginning actor is to attempt to motivate the entire speech as a single unit.

The following speech from *Golden Boy* contains at least twelve units, each of which needs a separate motivation. Joe Bonaparte, on the eve of his twenty-first birthday, is telling his father that he wants to break away from the economic and social restraints of home so that he may have "wonderful things from life." He thinks he can find what he wants by becoming a prize fighter. Mr. Bonaparte, a human and kindly man, has great hopes of Joe's finding happiness as a violinist. He has spent a good part of his savings to buy a fine violin which he plans to give Joe tomorrow for his birthday. Frank, Joe's older brother who travels about a good deal, is present. Also there is Mr. Carp, a neighbor who owns an *Encyclopaedia Britannica*.

MR. BONAPARTE. Sit down, Joe—resta you'self.

JOE. 1) Don't want to sit. 2) Every birthday I ever had I sat around. 3) Now'sa time for standing. 4) Poppa, I have to tell you—I don't like myself, past, present and future. 5) Do you know there are men who have wonderful things from life? 6) Do you think they're better than me? 7) Do you think I like this feeling of no possessions? 8) Of learning about the world from Carp's encyclopaedia? 9) Frank don't know what it means—he travels around, sees the world! 10) (*Turning to Frank*) You don't know what it means to sit around here and watch the months go ticking by! 11) Do you think that's a life for a boy my age? 12) Tomorrow's my birthday! I change my life! [3]

Joe's purpose in this speech as a whole is, of course, to inform his father that he is going to change his way of life and that the change will mean a difference in their relationship. His action-impulse is to break away from his home and his father. In spite of the fact that he is excited and resentful, he does not find it an easy thing to say, and he cannot say it all at once. Furthermore, he feels that it is necessary to defend his decision. Each part of the speech serves a different purpose in accomplishing his basic desire.

---

[3] Clifford Odets, *Golden Boy* (New York: Random House, Inc., 1937). Copyright, 1937, by Clifford Odets. Reprinted by permission of the publishers, Random House, Inc.

EXERCISES: The following speeches will provide material for practical work in interpreting the lines. Work successively on several of them. If possible, read the plays from which they have been selected carefully because the real significance of any single speech lies in its relationship to the play as a whole. Determine the motivating desire of the character. Break the speech into units. Find the action-impulse. Plan action that will help you to believe. Memorize the speech. Rehearse it for the purpose of motivating each unit separately and clearly relating the meaning of each unit to the basic desire expressed in the speech as a whole. If the language of the lines is different from your own, make a special study of the speech background of the character.

1) Trepleff in *The Sea Gull,* by Anton Chekhov.

(*Constantin Trepleff is an idealistic young man whose ambition to write for the theatre is constantly thwarted by his mother, a vain and frivolous actress. He is talking to a kindly and understanding uncle.*)

TREPLEFF. (*Picking petals from a flower*) Loves me—loves me not, loves me—loves me not, loves me—loves me not. (*Laughing*) You see, my mother doesn't love me, of course not. I should say not! What she wants is to live, and love, and wear pretty clothes; and here am I twenty-five years old and a perpetual reminder that she is no longer young. You see when I'm not there she's only thirty-two, and when I am she's forty-three—and for that she hates me. . . . I love my mother—I love her very much—but she leads a senseless life, always making a fuss over this novelist, her name forever chucked about in the papers—it disgusts me. It's just the simple egotism of an ordinary mortal, I suppose, stirring me up sometimes that makes me wish I had somebody besides a famous actress for a mother, and fancy if she'd been an ordinary woman I'd been happier. Uncle, can you imagine anything more hopeless than my position in her house? It used to be she'd entertain, all famous people—actors and authors —and among them all I was the only one who was nothing, and they put up with me only because I was her son. Who am I? What am I? I left the university in my third year, owing to circumstances, as they say, for which the editors are not responsible; I've no talent at all, not a kopeck on me; and according to my passport I am—a burgher of Kiev. My father was a burgher of Kiev, though he was also a famous actor. So when these actors and writers of hers bestowed on me their gracious attentions, it seemed to me their eyes were measuring my insignificance. I guessed their thoughts and felt humiliated.[4]

2) Marie in *Liliom*, by Ferenc Molnar.

(*Marie is a young servant girl who is wonderfully and happily in love. She is talking to Julie, a close friend of her own age.*)

MARIE. Yes. . . . He takes my hand and we walk along together. Then he wants to swing hands, but I won't let him. I say: "Don't swing my hand"; and he says, "Don't be so stubborn." And then he tries to swing my hand again, but I still don't let him. And for a long time I don't let him—until in the end I let him. Then we walk along swinging hands—up and down, up and down—just like this. *That* is Passionate Love. It's sinful, but it's awfully *thrilling.* . . . But the most beautiful thing is Ideal Love. . . . Daylight comes about three in the morning this time of year. When we've been up that long we're all through with flirting and Passionate Love—and then our Ideal Love comes to the surface. It comes like this: I'll be sitting on the bench and Wolf, he holds my hand tight —and he puts his cheek against my cheek and we don't talk . . . we just sit there very quiet. . . . And after a while he gets sleepy, and his head sinks down, and he falls asleep . . . but even in his sleep he holds tight to my hand. And I—I sit perfectly still just looking around me and taking long deep breaths—for by that time it's morning and the trees and flowers are fresh with dew. But Wolf doesn't smell anything because he's so fast asleep, but I don't sleep. And we sit like that for a long time. That is Ideal Love—[5]

3) Biff Loman in *Death of a Salesman*, by Arthur Miller.

(*Biff has just returned home after knocking aimlessly about the country for a number of years. He has no real object in life and no certain sense of values. He is talking to his brother.*)

BIFF. I tell ya, Hap, I don't know what my future is. I don't know—what I'm supposed to want. . . . I spent six or seven years

---

[4] Anton Chekhov, *The Sea Gull,* trans. by Stark Young (New York: Charles Scribner's Sons, 1939). Reprinted by permission of Charles Scribner's Sons.

[5] Ferenc Molnar, *Liliom,* trans. by Benjamin F. Glazer. Copyright, 1921, by United Plays, Inc. Reprinted by permission of Paramount Pictures Corporation.

after high school trying to work myself up. Shipping clerk, salesman, business of one kind or another. And it's a measly manner
of existence. To get on that subway on the hot mornings in summer. To devote your whole life to keeping stock, or making phone
calls, or selling or buying. To suffer fifty weeks of the year for the
sake of a two-week vacation, when all you really desire is to be outdoors, with your shirt off. And always to have to get ahead of the
next fella. And still—that's how you build a future. . . . Hap, I've
had twenty or thirty different kinds of jobs since I left home before
the war, and it always turns out the same. I just realized it lately.
In Nebraska when I herded cattle, and the Dakotas, and Arizona,
and now in Texas. It's why I came home now, I guess, because I
realized it. This farm I work on, it's spring there now, see? And
they've got about fifteen new colts. There's nothing more inspir-
ing or—beautiful than the sight of a mare and a new colt. And it's
cool there now, see? Texas is cool now, and it's spring. And
whenever spring comes to where I am, I suddenly get the feeling, my God, I'm not getting anywhere! What the hell am
I doing, playing around with horses, twenty-eight dollars a week!
I'm thirty-four years old, I oughta be makin' my future. That's
when I come running home. And now, I get here, and I don't know
what to do with myself. (*A pause*) I've always made a point of not
wasting my life, and every time I come back here I know that all
I've done is to waste my life.[6]

4) Mrs. Lincoln in *Abraham Lincoln*, by John Drinkwater.

(*The scene is the parlor of Abraham Lincoln's house in Spring-
field, Illinois, in 1860. Mrs. Lincoln is speaking to a group of
men who have come to offer her husband the nomination to the
Presidency of the United States.*)

MRS. LINCOLN. You have said this was a great evening for me.
It is, and I'll say more than I mostly do, because it is. I'm likely
to go into history now with a great man. For I know better than
any how great he is. I'm plain looking and I've a sharp tongue,
and I've a mind that doesn't always go in his easy, high way. And
that's what history will see, and it will laugh a little, and say, "Poor

⁶ Arthur Miller, *Death of a Salesman* (New York: The Viking Press, Inc.,
1949). Reprinted by permission of The Viking Press, Inc.

Abraham Lincoln." That's all right, but it's not all. I've always known when he should go forward, and when he should hold back. I've watched, and watched, and what I've learnt America will profit by. There are women like that, lots of them. But I'm lucky. My work's going farther than Illinois—it's going farther than any of us can tell. I made things easy for him to think and think when we were poor, and now his thinking has brought him to this. They wanted to make him Governor of Oregon, and he would have gone and come to nothing there. I stopped him. Now they're coming to ask him to be President, and I've told him to go.[7]

5) Christy Mahon in *The Playboy of the Western World*, by John Millington Synge.

(*A young Irishman named Christy Mahon, having run away from home, has been befriended by Pegeen Mike and her father, who owns a public house. Up early in the morning, Christy is polishing Pegeen's boots and counting the jugs behind the bar. He is speaking to himself.*)

CHRISTY. Half a hundred beyond. Ten there. A score that's above. Eighty jugs. Six cups and a broken one. Two plates. A power of glasses. Bottles, a schoolmaster'd be hard set to count, and enough in them, I'm thinking, to drunken all the wealth and wisdom of the County Clare. (*He puts the boot down carefully*) There's her boots, nice and decent for her evening use, and isn't it grand brushes she has? (*He puts them down and goes by degrees to the looking-glass*) Well, this'd be a fine place to be my whole life talking out with swearing Christians, in place of my old dogs and cat, and I stalking around, smoking my pipe and drinking my fill, and never a day's work but drawing a cork an odd time, or wiping a glass, or rinsing out a shiny tumbler for a decent man. (*He takes the looking-glass from the wall and puts it on the back of a chair; then sits down in front of it and begins washing his face*) Didn't I know rightly I was handsome, though it was the divil's own mirror we had beyond, would twist a squint across an angel's brow; and I'll be growing fine from this day, the way I'll have a soft lovely skin on me and won't be the like of the clumsy young fellows do be ploughing all times in the earth and dung. (*He starts*) Is she coming

---

[7] John Drinkwater, *Abraham Lincoln* (New York: Houghton Mifflin Co., 1919). Reprinted by permission of Houghton Mifflin Company.

again? (*He looks out*) Stranger girls. God help me, where'll I hide myself away and my long neck naked to the world. (*He looks out*) I'd best go to the room maybe till I'm dressed again. (*He gathers up his coat and looking-glass, and runs into the inner room*) [8]

6) Abbie Putnam in *Desire under the Elms*, by Eugene O'Neill.

(*Abbie is a young woman who has just married an old farmer named Ephraim Cabot. Here she is talking to Eben, Ephraim's grown-up son. He is strongly resentful of her.*)

ABBIE. (*Calmly*) If cussin' me does ye good, cuss all ye've a mind t'. I'm all prepared t' have you agin me—at fust. I don't blame ye nuther. I'd feel the same at any stranger comin' t' take my Maw's place. (*He shudders. She is watching him carefully*) Yew must've cared a lot fur yewr Maw, didn't ye? My Maw died afore I'd growed. I don't remember her none. (*A pause*) But yew won't hate me long, Eben. I'm not the wust in the world—an' ye an' me've got a lot in common. I kin tell that by lookin' at ye. Waal —I've had a hard life, too—oceans o' trouble an' nuthin' but wuk fur reward. I was an orphan early an' had t' work fur others in other folks' hums. Then I married an' he turned out a drunken spreer an' so he had to wuk fur others an' me too agen in other folks' hums, an' the baby died, an' my husband got sick an' died too, an' I was glad sayin' now I'm free fur once, on'y I diskivered right away all I was free fur was t' wuk agen in other folks' hums, doin' other folks' wuk till I'd most give up hope o' ever doin' my own wuk in my own hum, an' then your Paw come. . . . [9]

7) Juliet in *Romeo and Juliet*, by William Shakespeare.

(*Friar Laurence has given Juliet a potion which will keep her from having to marry Paris. It has the power to make her appear as dead. She will then remain in the family vault until Romeo comes from banishment to rescue her. In this scene, she has just said goodnight to her mother and her nurse, and is now alone realizing that she must drink the potion.*)

---

[8] John M. Synge, *The Playboy of the Western World*. Copyright, 1935, Modern Library, Inc. Reprinted by permission of Random House, Inc.

[9] Eugene O'Neill, *Desire under the Elms*. Copyright, 1925, by Eugene O'Neill. Reprinted by permission of Random House, Inc.

JULIET. Farewell! God knows when we shall meet again.
I have a faint cold fear thrills through my veins,
That almost freezes up the heat of life:
I'll call them back again to comfort me.
Nurse!—What should she do here?
My dismal scene I needs must act alone.
Come, vial.
What if this mixture do not work at all?
Shall I be married then tomorrow morning?
No, no; this shall forbid it. Lie thou there.

(Laying down a dagger)

What if it be a poison, which the friar
Subtly hath minister'd to have me dead,
Lest in this marriage he should be dishonor'd,
Because he married me before to Romeo?
I fear it is: and yet, methinks, it should not,
For he hath still been tried a holy man.
How if, when I am laid into the tomb,
I wake before the time that Romeo
Come to redeem me? there's a fearful point.
Shall I not then be stifled in the vault,
To whose foul mouth no healthsome air breathes in,
And there die strangled ere my Romeo comes?
Or, if I live, is it not very like,
The horrible conceit of death and night,
Together with the terror of the place,
As in a vault, an ancient receptacle,
Where for this many hundred years the bones
Of all my buried ancestors are pack'd;
Where bloody Tybalt, yet but green in earth,
Lies festering in his shroud; where, as they say,
At some hours in the night spirits resort;
Alack, alack, is it not like that I
So early waking, what with loathsome smells,
And shrieks like mandrakes' torn out of the earth,
That living mortals hearing them run mad:
O, if I wake, shall I not be distraught,
Environed with all these hideous fears?
And madly play with my forefathers' joints?

And pluck the mangled Tybalt from his shroud?
And, in this rage, with some great kinsman's bone,
As with a club, dash out my desperate brains?
O, look! methinks I see my cousin's ghost
Seeking out Romeo, that did spit his body
Upon a rapier's point: stay, Tybalt, stay!
Romeo, I come! this do I drink to thee.

> (*Falls upon the bed*)

8) Romeo in *Romeo and Juliet*, by William Shakespeare.

> (*Romeo, believing that Juliet is dead, comes to the tomb to poison himself.*)

ROMEO. How oft when men are at the point of death
Have they been merry! which their keepers call
A lightning before death: O, how may I
Call this a lightning? O my love! my wife!
Death, that has suck'd the honey of thy breath,
Hath had no power yet upon thy beauty:
Thou art not conquer'd; beauty's ensign yet
Is crimson in thy lips and in thy cheeks,
And death's pale flag is not advanced there.
Tybalt, liest thou there in thy bloody sheet?
O, what more favor can I do to thee
Than with that hand that cut thy youth in twain
To sunder his that was thine enemy?
Forgive me, cousin! Ah, dear Juliet,
Why art thou yet so fair? shall I believe
That unsubstantial death is amorous,
And that the lean abhorred monster keeps
Thee there in dark to be his paramour?
For fear of that, I still will stay with thee,
And never from this palace of dim night
Depart again: here, here will I remain
With worms that are thy chamber-maids; O, here
Will I set up my everlasting rest,
And shake the yoke of inauspicious stars
From this world-wearied flesh. Eyes, look your last!
Arms, take your last embrace! and, lips, O you

The doors of breath, seal with a righteous kiss
A dateless bargain to engrossing death!
Come, bitter conduct, come, unsavory guide!
Thou desperate pilot, now at once run on
The dashing rocks thy sea-sick weary bark.
Here's to my love. (*He drinks*) O true apothecary!
Thy drugs are quick. Thus with a kiss I die.

PART III

The Actor
and the Production

CHAPTER 11

Learning the Lingo

As soon as the actor begins rehearsals of a play that is being prepared for production, he has the advantage of working under the guidance of a director. The director, with a thorough knowledge of the values that the play contains and a technical resourcefulness in how to realize those values upon the stage, will be concerned with developing the characterizations of the individual actors to the point where they will make the greatest possible contribution in the expression of the total meaning of the play. He will be eager to help the actor create a character which is believable and which is true to the dramatist's intentions. He will also be concerned with making each actor an effective part of his master plan —a plan often intricately complicated in its detail—for coordinating all aspects of the production into an artistic whole. During the rehearsal period, he will give many directions to each actor. In so doing, he will use a standard stage terminology with which the actor must be familiar.

Like every profession, the theatre has its own special vocabulary. Partly technical, partly slang, it is generally standardized throughout the English-speaking theatre. It is as necessary for an actor to be familiar with this terminology as it is for a mechanic to know the names of his tools or for a surgeon to know the names of his instruments.

No effort will be made here to provide an exhaustive list of stage terms. At this point we need only those which an actor is certain to encounter in the process of receiving directions.[1]

1. STAGE DIRECTIONS

a) *Stage right.* The actor's right as he stands on the stage facing the audience.

b) *Stage left.* The actor's left as he stands on the stage facing the audience.

c) *Downstage.* Toward the audience.

d) *Upstage.* Away from the audience.

e) *Below.* Toward the audience. Same as "downstage of."

---

[1] For a more complete glossary of stage terminology, see Alexander Dean, *Fundamentals of Play Directing* (New York: Rinehart & Company, Inc., 1941), pp. 40–85, 385–413.

f) *Above.* Away from the audience. Same as "upstage of."

(An actor who walks *below* a piece of furniture walks between the furniture and the audience; an actor who walks *above* a piece of furniture walks between the furniture and the upstage wall of the setting.)

g) *In.* Toward the center of the stage.

h) *Out.* Away from the center of the stage.

(The direction to *move in 3 feet* means to move 3 feet closer to the center of the stage; to *move out 3 feet* means to move 3 feet further away from the center of the stage.)

2. STAGE AREAS

a) In order that a director may designate an actor's position on the stage precisely, the acting portion of the stage is divided into fifteen areas (see Drawing III).

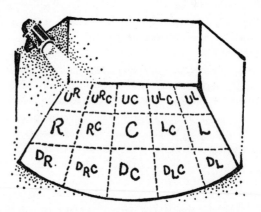

DRAWING III. *Stage Areas. These abbreviations stand for:*

Up Right, Up Right Center, Up Center, Up Left Center, Up Left.

Right, Right Center, Center, Left Center, Left.

Down Right, Down Right Center, Down Center, Down Left Center, Down Left.

b) *On stage.* That part of the stage enclosed by the setting which is visible to the audience in any particular scene.

c) *Off stage.* All parts of the stage not enclosed by the setting.

d) *Backstage.* Usually the entire stage portion of the theatre building in contrast to the auditorium which is designated as *out front.*

e) *Wings.* Offstage space at right and left of the acting areas.

3. BODY POSITIONS

a) In order to designate the position the actor is facing in relation to the audience, there are eight *body positions* (see Drawing IV).

b) *Open.* An "open" position is one in which the actor is facing toward the audience, or nearly so. To "open" is to turn toward the audience.

c) *Closed.* A "closed" position is one in which the actor is turned away from the audience. To "close in" is to turn away from the audience.

4. ACTORS' POSITIONS IN RELATION TO EACH OTHER

Actors' positions in relation to each other are considered with regard to the relative emphasis each actor receives.

a) *Share.* Two actors *share* a scene when they are both "open" to an equal degree, thus allowing the audience to see them equally well (see Drawing V).

b) *Give, take.* When two actors are not equally "open" and one receives a greater emphasis than the other, the actor emphasized is said to *take* the scene. The other is said to *give* the scene (see Drawing VI).

5. STAGE MOVEMENT

a) *Cross.* Movement from one area to another. In writing it is generally abbreviated by *X*.

b) *Blocking.* The term applied to the process of working out the actor's movements and positions during rehearsal.

c) *Cover.* An actor is said to be *covered* when another actor moves into a position between him and the audience, thus obstructing him from view. Covering is usually to be avoided.

d) *Dress stage.* A direction requesting the actors to adjust their positions in order to improve the compositional effect of the stage picture.

6. STAGE BUSINESS

Small actions, such as smoking, eating, using a fan, tying a necktie, are known on the stage as "business."

Full Back

Three Quarters Right

Three Quarters Left

Profile Right

Profile Left

One Quarter Right

One Quarter Left

Full Front

DRAWING IV. *Body Positions*

DRAWING V. *Shared Positions*

7. PROPERTIES

Business often involves the use of properties. "Props," as they are commonly called, are divided into several categories.

a) *Hand props.* Small objects which the actors handle on stage such as teacups, letters, books, candies.

b) *Personal props.* Hand props carried on the actor's person and used only by him such as watches, spectacles, cigarette holders. An actor is usually responsible for taking care of his personal props during rehearsals and performances.

c) *Costume props.* Costume accessories used by the actor in executing business such as fans, walking sticks, gloves, handbags.

d) *Stage props.* Objects for dressing the stage which are not used by the actors in executing their business. Vases of flowers, lamps, clocks, bric-a-brac might be stage props.

8. TERMS REGARDING LINES AND DIALOGUE

a) *Ad lib.* Coming from the Latin *ad libitum* (at pleasure), the term applies to lines supplied by the actor wherever they may be required

DRAWING VI. *Given and Taken Positions*

as in crowd scenes or to fill in where there would otherwise be an undesirable pause.

b) *Aside.* A line which the other actors on stage are not supposed to be hearing. The aside was a regular convention in plays of the seventeenth, eighteenth, and nineteenth centuries. It is rarely used by modern dramatists.

c) *Build.* To increase the tempo and/or volume in order to reach a climax.

d) *Cue.* The last words of a speech, or the end of an action, indicating the time for another actor to speak or act. An actor must memorize his cues just as carefully as he memorizes his lines.

e) *Drop.* Lines on which the actor does not project his voice sufficiently to be heard are said to be *dropped.* The direction in such a case is usually, "Don't drop your lines."

f) *Pick up cues.* A direction for the actor to begin speaking immediately at the end of the cue without allowing any lapse of time. Beginning actors tend to be slow in picking up cues with the result that they often fail to maintain a tempo fast enough to hold the interest of the audience.

g) *Tag line.* The last line of a scene or act immediately before the lowering of the curtain.

h) *Top.* To "build" a line higher than the one that preceded it.

9. SOME MISCELLANEOUS TERMS

a) *Act drop.* A drop curtain lowered at the end of acts. Often it is a drop especially painted for a particular play.

b) *Apron.* The part of the stage that extends toward the audience in front of the curtain. Also termed *forestage.*

c) *Asbestos.* The fireproof curtain that closes the proscenium opening and separates the stage from the auditorium in case of fire.

d) *Back drop.* The drop furthest upstage in any setting.

e) *Backing.* A drop or flats used outside an opening in the setting such as a door or window.

f) *Bit part.* A small part with few lines.

g) *Call board.* A backstage bulletin board on which notices of concern to the actors are posted.

h) *Clear stage.* A direction given by the stage manager for everyone not immediately involved to leave the stage preparatory to the beginning of an act or to striking the setting.

i) *Curtain line.* The imaginary line across the stage floor which the front curtain touches when it is closed.

j) *Flats.* The canvas-covered frames which constitute the walls of a stage setting.

k) *Flies.* The space above the stage in which scenery is suspended.

l) *Front curtain.* A curtain closing the proscenium opening which hangs immediately behind the asbestos. It is usually used as the act drop.

m) *Green room.* A room located close to the stage in which the actors may await entrance cues.

n) *Gridiron.* A contrivance located in the flies for suspending scenery.

o) *Places.* A direction given by the stage manager for everyone to be in his proper position for the beginning of an act.

p) *Proscenium.* The wall dividing the stage from the auditorium.

q) *Proscenium opening.* The arched opening through which the audience sees the stage.

r) *Strike.* The direction given by the stage manager to change the setting for another scene or to dismantle it at the end of a performance.

s) *Trap.* An opening in the stage floor.

t) *Walk-on.* A small part without lines.

Acting in the Round

There is an increasing popularity throughout the country for theatre-in-the-round—also called "arena staging" or "central staging." This method of production, in which a centrally located acting area is surrounded by the audience, demands in some instances its own terminology. The vocabulary of the picture-frame stage having to do with direction and position (stage right and left, up and down, one quarter right, and so forth) does not apply because the actor and the audience are in a different relationship.

Central staging is a comparatively recent method of production in the modern theatre. So far no vocabulary for it has come into general use. There is a practice of designating acting areas in either one of two ways: according to the points of the compass (see Drawing VII) or according to the hours of the clock (see Drawing VIII). Thus, an actor may be directed to cross either to "northwest" or to "ten o'clock."

Theatre-in-the-round is truly an "actors' theatre." Since it cannot use standing scenery, nor make as extensive use as the proscenium theatre of many kinds of stage effects, the actor bears a greater responsibility for communicating the play to the audience.

There is, however, no basic difference in creating a character in arena and on the proscenium stage. Such differences as exist between the two approaches are the result of the actor's having to make technical adjustments to different actor-audience relationships. The actor in arena must be heard and seen from all sides rather than from one. The closeness of the audience, the fact that spectators sitting in the front row are usually not more than a couple of feet from the acting area, may be a

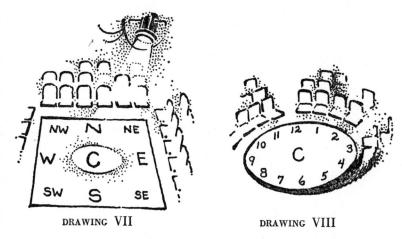

DRAWING VII   DRAWING VIII

Acting Areas in Arena

distracting influence and add an additional complication to the problem of concentration. Furthermore, this same closeness makes an especially exacting demand for maintaining an unwavering belief throughout the performance.[2]

---

[2] For a detailed description of arena theatre see Margo Jones, *Theatre-in-the-Round* (New York: Rinehart & Company, Inc., 1951).

CHAPTER 12

Rehearsing the Play

During the rehearsal period the actor works with the director, with the other actors, and, finally, with the various production crews. Everyone involved is working toward a single objective—the expression of the total meaning of a particular play. Everyone is a part of a complicated cooperative enterprise. Although they often are not sharply defined, and there may be considerable overlapping, there are five principal phases in the process of rehearsing a play:

1) finding the meaning,
2) blocking the movement,
3) developing the characters,
4) making technical adjustments,
5) polishing for performance.

Finding the Meaning

If the production of a play is actually to realize its full possibilities, if it is to be the "relating of a number of talents to a single meaning" (see Chapter 9), then everyone working on the production must understand what that single meaning is. And everyone must understand further how his particular part, small or large as it may be, contributes to the expression of it. That part of the rehearsal period devoted to finding the meaning of the play is of fundamental importance.

There are a number of different ways in which the director, the actors, and the designers may come to an agreement about the meaning. An understanding may be reached in group discussion, each person having carefully analyzed the play beforehand, being ready to present his own interpretation, and being willing to modify it if necessary. The director, possibly having a more thorough knowledge of the play than anyone else, may teach his interpretation to the others. Or agreement may be reached through a combination of these approaches. A common procedure is a number of "reading rehearsals" in which actors sit in a circle reading aloud their individual parts and discussing the play with the director and with each other.

The important thing is that everyone clearly understand what the play means. Until this common understanding has been reached, the

132

group is likely to be working at cross purposes and rehearsals cannot proceed effectively.

As soon as an interpretation of the play as a whole has been agreed upon, each individual actor will search for the basic motivating desire of the character he is playing and the relationship of this desire to the total meaning of the play. Here again discussion is in order. Agreement on this point between the actor and the director is necessary before rehearsals may proceed effectively. Usually, an understanding is reached during reading rehearsals. At the same time, the actor begins to consider the problem of line interpretation—of relating the lines to the character's motivating desire and to the meaning of the play as a whole.

The amount of time given to finding the meaning through reading and discussion may vary from one or two rehearsals to as much as one third of the entire rehearsal period, depending upon the practice of the director and the subtleties of the play.

Blocking the Movement

As soon as the meaning of the play is thoroughly understood, rehearsals continue with blocking of the movement. The director will explain in detail the "ground plan" of the setting that he and the scene designer have agreed upon. Using a model or a scale drawing, he will describe the locations of the exits and entrances, the placement of the furniture, the position of any steps and levels that may be used. The actor should make a diagram of the ground plan in his script. Once it has been explained, the actor is responsible for knowing it.

More than one procedure is possible in blocking the actor's large movements (that is, his exits and entrances, and his crosses from one area of the stage to another). The actor and the director may work them out entirely in rehearsal, thus allowing the actor considerable freedom in finding movement which he feels is right and true for the character. Often the large movements are given the actor by the director who has carefully planned them in advance of the rehearsal in relation to the character's motivating desires and in relation to a compositional pattern that will express the meaning of the play as a whole. In such cases as this, the actor accepts the movement planned by the director in the same way that he accepts the lines provided by the dramatist. No matter what the procedure, it is necessary that the actor be able to justify the movement in terms of the character's wants. Otherwise, no movement has any reason for being.

Once the movement has been given by the director, or once it has been worked out by the director and the actor at rehearsal, an actor is responsible for remembering his blocking. He should clearly indicate all stage movement in the margin of his script *at the time the movement is blocked at rehearsal.* Such abbreviations as these are convenient:

Sit ULC
X DRC below sofa
Exit DL

Drawing small diagrams in the margin of the script is also a practical way of recording movement (see Drawing IX).

DRAWING IX

There is always a certain amount of movement inherent in the lines of a play, such as the exits and entrances, crossing to answer the doorbell or the telephone, serving tea, and so forth. The dramatist may also suggest other movement in his stage directions. It is always necessary, however, for the actor to have additional movement. He needs as many physical objectives as possible to give him a belief in his character and, also, to provide an opportunity of expressing the desires of the character in movement which the audience can *see* and understand.

Developing the Character

With the meaning of the play thoroughly in mind and with the stage movement blocked, the actor is ready to concentrate on further details of characterization. It is during this part of the rehearsal period that he may find greatest satisfaction in his function as a creative artist. It is at this time that he *explores* his inner resources to discover how he can use his own experiences to bring understanding and sympathy to the problems of the character he is playing. It is at this time that he *uses his imagination* to supply additional circumstances which will round out the character's background and aid him in believing the action. It is at this time that he *observes* people and objects around him to find details which help him in his characterization.

It is also during this part of the rehearsal period that the actor decides upon what *externals* of manner, of dress, of action, and so forth, will aid him in believing the character. An important part of this aspect of character development is determining the "business" he will use in his performance. Business is vital in characterization because, as we recall from earlier chapters, *doing is believing*. The actor is likely to believe his character to the extent that he is able to translate the character's desires into action. Such small actions as using a handkerchief, eating a sandwich, writing down an address, flicking a bit of dust from one's coat sleeve, provide physical objectives upon which the actor can concentrate his attention. Determining the amount and nature of the business is a matter to be settled between the actor and the director. The director frequently makes suggestions. The actor, however, has both the opportunity and the responsibility of originating small actions which will help him to believe his character. All business, like the lines and the stage movement, must be justified in terms of the character's motivating desire.

At the same time the actor is working on his lines. He is studying them carefully to determine the motivation behind each line, to discover the under-meaning and the action-impulse, and to relate them to the character's basic motivating desire. He is concerning himself with the background of the character's speech. If the background differs from his own, he is learning to reproduce the speech truthfully and believably by listening to speakers with a similar background or to phonograph records. He is also memorizing his lines and cues.

Among professional actors practice in memorization varies widely. Lynn Fontanne has said that she has her lines completely memorized before she begins rehearsals so she is free to concentrate entirely upon problems of character development. Alla Nazimova said that she never memorized her lines. She "absorbed" them as she developed her character. She came finally to understand her role so thoroughly that she could *think* the lines as the playwright had written them without ever having actually committed them to memory.[1]

Both of these practices are extremes. There are dangers in memorizing the lines before the rehearsals begin. Without having had the oppor-

---

[1] For a description of the working methods of these and several other prominent modern actors see Morton Eustis, *Players at Work* (New York: Theatre Arts Books, 1937).

tunity of discussing the play with the director and other members of the cast, there is always the possibility of forming opinions which are incorrect or, at least, at odds with the interpretation decided upon by the group as a whole. Once the actor has learned the lines, it would be doubly difficult for him to modify the pattern of thought that had become established. Gradual absorption of the lines is a time-consuming process. And anyone with a less superb technique than Mme. Nazimova's can hardly rely upon coming to think the lines without having memorized them— admirable as the theory may be. Accurate memorization is another of the actor's responsibilities. He owes it to the dramatist who is dependent upon the actor for a truthful representation of his work. He owes it also to his fellow players whose own lines must be motivated by what has gone before.

As a general practice a policy of memorization somewhere between these two extremes is advisable. After the actor is familiar with the meaning of the play and with the motivating desire of his character, he will not establish incorrect interpretations while he is memorizing his lines. After the movement has been blocked, the lines may be associated with the movement which is likely in many instances to clarify their meaning and to make the memorization easier. Circumstances may alter cases, but generally it is wise to have the lines completely memorized at the halfway point of the entire rehearsal period. This time schedule allows the actor to gain advantage from the earlier rehearsals, and it insures his freedom from the burden of memorization during the final stages of preparation.

Making Technical Adjustments

Somewhere toward the end of the rehearsal period the actors begin to work in the setting, with the actual properties that will be used in performance, in costume, and under the lights. At this time some adjustments are almost always necessary. The furniture may take up more space than the small chairs and tables the actors have been working with. Opening and closing actual doors may require more time than the actors have been allowing in pantomime. The position of a piano may have to be changed to improve the sight lines for the audience. The manipulation of the costumes may require more care than has been anticipated. A climactic scene may have to be played further down stage in order that it may be lighted effectively. Certain actions may have to be repeated over and over to allow the lighting and sound crews to coordinate their timing with that of the actors.

Such adjustments are an inevitable part of the rehearsal period. They are necessary to provide a production which will most fully realize the possibilities of the play. For a short time they may interfere with the actor's concentration and prevent him from believing the action he is performing. For the experienced actor, however, the period of uncertainty and discomfort is brief. He recognizes the necessity for the changes, and he immediately finds ways (sometimes by inventing additional "circumstances") to motivate them in terms of the desires of his character.

Polishing for Performance

The final rehearsals are devoted to polishing the play for performance. At this time experimentation ceases. Any feeling of tentativeness that may have existed in regard to the details of the production is eliminated. The actor has had ample opportunity during the earlier rehearsals to try out different ways of bringing his character into existence upon the stage. He has experimented (always under the guidance and subject to the approval of the director) with various details of business, movement, and line reading. Throughout the entire rehearsal period he has been deciding what details will help him in believing his character. There has been, in fact, a continual process of selection and rejection. By the time the play is ready to be polished for performance final choices must have been made. During the final rehearsals the actor needs to be confident that all problems of characterization, as well as all technical problems of production, have been solved to the best of everyone's ability. Only then can he become comfortable and assured in his performance.

Although both will have been anticipated earlier, the principal considerations in the process of polishing are *timing* and *projection*.

Timing is a matter of pace and rhythm. It has to do with the tempo at which the lines are spoken, at which the business and the movement are executed, and with the rapidity at which the cues are picked up. A tempo cannot be established and maintained as long as the actors feel any uncertainty about any details of their performance.

A sense of timing is one of the most subtle elements of stage technique. It is an element which demands for its development that the actor have experience before an audience. Too slow a tempo will not hold the interest of an audience. Too fast a tempo will obscure the meaning. Too consistent a tempo will become monotonous. Too varied a tempo will seem jerky and illogical.

The beginning actor often tends to be slow in picking up his cues with the result that the rhythm falters between speeches. On the other hand, he often tends to be too fast in speaking the lines with the result that the meaning is blurred—a clear indication that he is not thinking and believing what he is saying. He tends to maintain too constant a tempo with the result that he does not make use of variations in pace to express variations in mood. He tends to be afraid of pauses and, consequently, loses one of the most effective ways of emphasizing important lines and actions.

Timing varies from play to play, from scene to scene, from character to character, and from audience to audience. The thought-provoking play requires a slower tempo than the farce comedy. Expository scenes at the beginning of the play require a slower tempo than climactic scenes at the end. One character moves and speaks more slowly than another. One audience is quicker at grasping meanings than another. During the final rehearsals, the director will guide the actor in establishing tempos which will be effective for the play, for the different scenes, for the different characters. The actors alone have the responsibility of *feeling out* the audience and making such adjustments in timing as may be necessary.

Projection is another variable element. The constant requirement is that everyone in the audience be able to hear and understand the lines. This requirement may be satisfied, however, in a wide variety of voices ranging from a shout to a whisper. The particular degree of loudness which is most suitable must be determined by the play, the scene, the character, the size and acoustical qualities of the auditorium. Again, a certain amount of variety throughout the performance is necessary. Nothing is more tiresome than listening over a period of time to an unvaried voice. Too abrupt changes in volume, on the other hand, are likely to startle the audience, to attract undue attention; and, of even greater importance, they may rarely be justified in terms of the character's desires.

There must be visual projection, as well as auditory. The audience must *see* and understand the action as clearly as they *hear* and understand the lines. Three requirements of movement, business, and gesture are

1) that they be suitable to the character, the scene, the play, and the general style of the production;

2) that they be clearly seen; and

3) that their significance in terms of the character's motivating desire be readily comprehensible.

At the final rehearsals, actors need to be especially concerned with the effectiveness of their auditory and visual projection. The director will be especially careful to check its effectiveness at all points of the performance. It is largely to insure that the meaning of the play will be adequately projected on opening night that New York producers have out of town tryouts. It is for the same reason that noncommercial directors either have preview performances or invite audiences to the final "run-throughs."

CHAPTER 13

Playing the Part

From the foregoing discussion of rehearsal procedure, it is apparent that during the first part of the rehearsal period the actor is concerned almost entirely with coming to understand the character he is playing, and of coming to believe the character's speech and actions. Later he becomes increasingly concerned with finding ways of projecting the character to the audience. During performance, the actor is concerned with both characterization and projection. He must bring the character into existence upon the stage. He must also project the character to the audience with whatever "comment" the play and the production demand.

Concentration is the keynote to success during performance. And the actor concentrates throughout upon *two levels.*

On the one level he directs his attention to satisfying the desires of the character he is playing. Through his speech and action he attempts to get what the character wants. He attempts to influence the behavior of the other characters for the purpose of satisfying his objective. In concentrating on the accomplishment of this objective he comes to have an imaginary belief in his actions which produces, in turn, imaginary feelings similar, if not identical, to the feelings the character would have if the situations were actually in life.

On another level the actor is concentrating on expressing this character in theatrical terms. The lines must be heard. The actions must be seen. A tempo must be maintained which will be suitable to the play, stimulating to the audience, and dramatically effective. Throughout the performance, all the elements must have enough variety to insure a continual renewal of interest. The character must be presented to draw forth from the audience the response which the dramatist intended.

Moreover, the successful actor must serve in his dual function of character and interpreter with apparent ease and with a sense of authority. There is no pleasure in watching a performer who is tense and strained, and there is no comfort in watching one who does not appear confident in his ability to get through the performance with some degree of credit to himself. Concentration, again, is the keynote to relaxation. When the actor can turn his full attention to doing a job he knows he is prepared to do, he forgets his fears and his self-consciousness. He "turns to" with a directness and an energy which are requisite to his success.

It has been the purpose of this book to help the beginning actor to gain such ease and confidence.

APPENDIX

Short Plays

for Study and
Practice

THE PROPOSAL [1]

by *Anton Chekhov*

CHARACTERS

STEPAN STEPANOVITCH CHUBUKOV, a landowner.
NATALYA STEPANOVNA, his daughter, twenty-five years old.
IVAN VASSILEVITCH LOMOV, a neighbor of Chubukov, a large and hearty,
but very suspicious landowner.

The scene is laid at CHUBUKOV's *country house.*

LOMOV *enters, wearing a dress-jacket and white gloves.* CHUBUKOV *rises to meet him.*

CHUBUKOV. My dear fellow, whom do I see! Ivan Vassilevitch! I am extremely glad! (*Squeezes his hand*) Now this is a surprise, my darling. . . . How are you?

LOMOV. Thank you. And how may you be getting on?

CHUBUKOV. We just get along somehow, my angel, thanks to your prayers, and so on. Sit down, please do. . . . Now, you know, you shouldn't forget all about your neighbours, my darling. My dear fellow, why are you so formal in your get-up? Evening dress, gloves, and so on. Can you be going anywhere, my treasure?

LOMOV. No, I've come only to see you, honoured Stepan Stepanovitch.

CHUBUKOV. Then why are you in evening dress, my precious? As if you're paying a New Year's Eve visit!

LOMOV. Well, you see, it's like this. (*Takes his arm*) I've come to you, honoured Stepan Stepanovitch, to trouble you with a request. Not once or twice have I already had the privilege of applying to you for help, and you have always, so to speak. . . . I must ask your pardon, I am getting excited. I shall drink some water, honoured Stepan Stepanovitch. (*Drinks*)

---

[1] From *The Plays of Anton Chekhov* (New York: World Publishing Company, 1935). Copyright by Illustrated Editions, Inc., 1935. Reprinted by permission of Avon Publications, Inc.

CHUBUKOV. (*Aside*) He's come to borrow money! Shan't give him any! (*Aloud*) What is it, my beauty?

LOMOV. You see, Honour Stepanitch. . . . I beg pardon, Stepan Honouritch. . . . I mean, I'm awfully excited, as you will please notice. . . . In short, you alone can help me, though I don't deserve it, of course . . . and haven't any right to count on your assistance . . . .

CHUBUKOV. Oh, don't go round and round it, darling! Spit it out! Well?

LOMOV. One moment . . . this very minute. The fact is, I've come to ask the hand of your daughter, Natalya Stepanovna, in marriage.

CHUBUKOV. (*Joyfully*) By Jove! Ivan Vassilevitch! Say it again— I didn't hear it all!

LOMOV. I have the honour to ask . . .

CHUBUKOV. (*Interrupting*) My dear fellow . . . I'm so glad, and so on. . . . Yes, indeed, and all that sort of thing. (*Embraces and kisses* LOMOV) I've been hoping for it for a long time. It's been my continual desire. (*Sheds a tear*) And I've always loved you, my angel, as if you were my own son. May God give you both His help and His love and so on, and I did so much hope. . . . What am I behaving in this idiotic way for? I'm off balance with joy, absolutely off my balance! Oh, with all my soul. . . . I'll go and call Natasha, and all that.

LOMOV. (*Greatly moved*) Honoured Stepan Stepanovitch, do you think I may count on her consent?

CHUBUKOV. Why, of course, my darling, and . . . as if she won't consent! She's in love; egad, she's like a love-sick cat, and so on . . . . Shan't be long! (*Exit*)

LOMOV. It's cold . . . I'm trembling all over, just as if I'd got an examination before me. The great thing is, I must have my mind made up. If I give myself time to think, to hesitate, to talk a lot, to look for an ideal, or for real love, then I'll never get married. . . . Brr! . . . It's cold! Natalya Stepanovna is an excellent house-keeper, not bad-looking, well-educated. . . . What more do I want? But I'm getting a noise in my ears from excitement. (*Drinks*) And it's impossible for me not to marry. . . . In the first place, I'm already 35—a critical age, so to speak. In the second place, I ought to lead a quiet and regular life. . . . I suffer from palpitations, I'm excitable and always getting awfully upset. . . . At this very moment my lips are trembling, and there's a twitch in my right eyebrow. . . . But the very worst of all is the way I sleep. I no sooner get into bed and begin to go off when suddenly something in my left side—gives a pull, and I can feel it in my shoulder and head. . . . I jump up like a lunatic, walk about a bit, and lie down again, but as soon as I begin to get off to sleep there's another pull! And this may happen twenty times. . . .

NATALYA STEPANOVNA *comes in.*

NATALYA STEPANOVNA. Well, there! It's you, and papa said, "Go; there's a merchant come for his goods!" How do you do, Ivan Vassilevitch!

LOMOV. How do you do, honoured Natalya Stepanovna?

NATALYA STEPANOVNA. You must excuse my apron and house dress . . . we're shelling peas for drying. Why haven't you been here for such a long time? Sit down. . . . (*They seat themselves*) Won't you have some lunch?

LOMOV. No, thank you, I've had some already.

NATALYA STEPANOVNA. Then smoke. . . . Here are the matches. . . . The weather is splendid now, but yesterday it was so wet that the workmen didn't do anything all day. How much hay have you stacked? Just think, I felt greedy and had a whole field cut, and now I'm not at all pleased about it because I'm afraid my hay may rot. I ought to have waited a bit. But what's this? Why, you're in evening dress! Well, I never! Are you going to a ball, or what?—though I must say you look better. . . . Tell me, why are you got up like that?

LOMOV. (*Excited*) You see, honoured Natalya Stepanovna . . . the fact is, I've made up my mind to ask you to hear me out. . . . Of course you'll be surprised and perhaps even angry, but a . . . (*Aside*) It's awfully cold!

NATALYA STEPANOVNA. What's the matter? (*Pause*) Well?

LOMOV. I shall try to be brief. You must know, honoured Natalya Stepanovna, that I have long, since my childhood, in fact, had the privilege of knowing your family. My late aunt and her husband, from whom, as you know, I inherited my land, always had the greatest respect for your father and your late mother. The Lomovs and the Chubukovs have always had the most friendly, and I might almost say the most affectionate, regard for each other. And, as you know, my land is a near neighbour of yours. You will remember that my Oxen Meadows touch your birchwoods.

NATALYA STEPANOVNA. Excuse my interrupting you. You say, "My Oxen Meadows . . . ." But are they yours?

LOMOV. Yes, mine.

NATALYA STEPANOVNA. What are you talking about? Oxen Meadows are ours, not yours!

LOMOV. No, mine, honoured Natalya Stepanovna.

NATALYA STEPANOVNA. Well, I never knew that before. How do you make that out?

LOMOV. How? I'm speaking of those Oxen Meadows which are wedged in between your birchwoods and the Burnt Marsh.

NATALYA STEPANOVNA. Yes, yes. . . . They're ours.

LOMOV. No, you're mistaken, honoured Natalya Stepanovna, they're mine.

NATALYA STEPANOVNA. Just think, Ivan Vassilevitch! How long have they been yours?

LOMOV. How long? As long as I can remember.

NATALYA STEPANOVNA. Really, you won't get me to believe that!

LOMOV. But you can see from the documents, honoured Natalya Stepanovna. Oxen Meadows, it's true, were once the subject of dispute, but now everybody knows that they are mine. There's nothing to argue about. You see, my aunt's grandmother gave the free use of these Meadows in perpetuity to the peasants of your father's grandfather, in return for which they were to make bricks for her. The peasants belonging to your father's grandfather had the free use of the Meadows for forty years, and had got into the habit of regarding them as their own, when it happened that . . .

NATALYA STEPANOVNA. No, it isn't at all like that! Both my grandfather and great-grandfather reckoned that their land extended to Burnt Marsh—which means that Oxen Meadows were ours. I don't see what there is to argue about. It's simply silly!

LOMOV. I'll show you the documents, Natalya Stepanovna!

NATALYA STEPANOVNA. No, you're simply joking, or making fun of me. . . . What a surprise! We've had the land for nearly three hundred years, and then we're suddenly told that it isn't ours! Ivan Vassilevitch, I can hardly believe my own ears. . . . These Meadows aren't worth much to me. They only come to five dessiatins,* and are worth perhaps 300 roubles,† but I can't stand unfairness. Say what you will, but I can't stand unfairness.

LOMOV. Hear me out, I implore you! The peasants of your father's grandfather, as I have already had the honour of explaining to you,

* 13½ acres.
† 30 pounds.

used to bake bricks for my aunt's grandmother. Now my aunt's grandmother, wishing to make them a pleasant . . .

NATALYA STEPANOVNA. I can't make head or tail of all this about
aunts and grandfathers and grandmothers. The Meadows are ours, and
that's all.

LOMOV. Mine.

NATALYA STEPANOVNA. Ours! You can go on proving it for two days
on end, you can go and put on fifteen dress-jackets, but I tell you they're
ours, ours, ours! I don't want anything of yours and I don't want to give
up anything of mine. So there!

LOMOV. Natalya Stepanovna, I don't want the Meadows, but I am acting on principle. If you like, I'll make you a present of them.

NATALYA STEPANOVNA. I can make you a present of them myself, because they're mine. Your behaviour, Ivan Vassilevitch, is strange, to say
the least! Up to this we have always thought of you as a good neighbour,
a friend; last year we lent you our threshing-machine, although on that
account we had to put off our own threshing till November, but you behave to us as if we were gipsies. Giving me my own land, indeed! No,
really, that's not at all neighbourly! In my opinion, it's even impudent,
if you want to know. . . .

LOMOV. Then you make out that I'm a land-grabber? Madam, never
in my life have I grabbed anybody else's land, and I shan't allow anybody to accuse me of having done so. . . . (*Quickly steps to the carafe
and drinks more water*) Oxen Meadows are mine!

NATALYA STEPANOVNA. It's not true, they're ours!

LOMOV. Mine!

NATALYA STEPANOVNA. It's not true! I'll prove it! I'll send my mowers out to the Meadows this very day!

LOMOV. What?

NATALYA STEPANOVNA. My mowers will be there this very day!

LOMOV. I'll give it to them in the neck!

NATALYA STEPANOVNA. You dare!

LOMOV. (*Clutches at his heart*) Oxen Meadows are mine! You understand? Mine!

NATALYA STEPANOVNA. Please don't shout! You can shout yourself
hoarse in your own house, but here I must ask you to restrain yourself!

LOMOV. If it wasn't, madam, for this awful, excruciating palpitation, if my whole inside wasn't upset, I'd talk to you in a different way!
(*Yells*) Oxen Meadows are mine!

NATALYA STEPANOVNA. Ours!

LOMOV. Mine!

NATALYA STEPANOVNA. Ours!

LOMOV. Mine!

Enter CHUBUKOV.

CHUBUKOV. What's the matter? What are you shouting at?

NATALYA STEPANOVNA. Papa, please tell this gentleman who owns Oxen Meadows, we or he?

CHUBUKOV. (*To* LOMOV) Darling, the Meadows are ours!

LOMOV. But, please, Stepan Stepanovitch, how can they be yours? Do be a reasonable man! My aunt's grandmother gave the Meadows for the temporary and free use of your grandfather's peasants. The peasants used the land for forty years and got as accustomed to it as if it was their own, when it happened that . . .

CHUBUKOV. Excuse me, my precious . . . . You forget just this, that the peasants didn't pay your grandmother and all that, because the Meadows were in dispute, and so on. And now everybody knows that they're ours. It means that you haven't seen the plan.

LOMOV. I'll prove to you that they're mine!

CHUBUKOV. You won't prove it, my darling.

LOMOV. I shall!

CHUBUKOV. Dear one, why yell like that? You won't prove anything by just yelling. I don't want anything of yours, and don't intend to give up what I have. Why should I? And you know, my beloved, that if you propose to go on arguing about it, I'd much sooner give up the Meadows to the peasants than to you. There!

LOMOV. I don't understand! How have you the right to give away somebody else's property?

CHUBUKOV. You may take it that I know whether I have the right or not. Because, young man, I'm not used to being spoken to in that tone of voice, and so on: I, young man, am twice your age, and ask you to speak to me without agitating yourself, and all that.

LOMOV. No, you just think I'm a fool and want to have me on! You call my land yours, and then you want me to talk to you calmly and politely! Good neighbours don't behave like that, Stepan Stepanovitch! You're not a neighbour, you're a grabber!

CHUBUKOV. What's that? What did you say?

NATALYA STEPANOVNA. Papa, send the mowers out to the Meadows at once!

CHUBUKOV. What did you say, sir?

NATALYA STEPANOVNA. Oxen Meadows are ours, and I shan't give them up, shan't give them up, shan't give them up!

LOMOV. We'll see! I'll have the matter taken to court, and then I'll show you!

CHUBUKOV. To court? You can take it to court, and all that! You can! I know you; you're just on the look-out for a chance to go to court, and all that. . . . You pettifogger! All your people were like that! All of them!

LOMOV. Never mind about my people! The Lomovs have all been honourable people, and not one has ever been tried for embezzlement, like your grandfather!

CHUBUKOV. You Lomovs have had lunacy in your family, all of you!

NATALYA STEPANOVNA. All, all, all!

CHUBUKOV. Your grandfather was a drunkard, and your younger aunt, Nastasya Mihailovna, ran away with an architect, and so on. . . .

LOMOV. And your mother was hump-backed. (*Clutches at his heart*) Something pulling in my side. . . . My head. . . . Help! Water!

CHUBUKOV. Your father was a guzzling gambler!

NATALYA STEPANOVNA. And there haven't been many backbiters to equal your aunt!

LOMOV. My left foot has gone to sleep. . . . You're an intriguer. . . . Oh, my heart! . . . And it's an open secret that before the last elections you bri . . . I can see stars. . . . Where's my hat?

NATALYA STEPANOVNA. It's low! It's dishonest! It's mean!

CHUBUKOV. And you're just a malicious, double-faced intriguer! Yes!

LOMOV. Here's my hat. . . . My heart! . . . Which way? Where's the door? Oh! . . . I think I'm dying. . . . My foot's quite numb. . . . (*Goes to the door*)

CHUBUKOV. (*Following him*) And don't set foot in my house again!

NATALYA STEPANOVNA. Take it to court! We'll see!

LOMOV *staggers out.*

CHUBUKOV. Devil take him! (*To table for drink*)

Walks about in excitement.

NATALYA STEPANOVNA. What a rascal! What trust can one have in one's neighbours after that!

CHUBUKOV. The villain! The scarecrow! (*Down L.*)

NATALYA STEPANOVNA. The monster! First he takes our land and then he has the impudence to abuse us.

CHUBUKOV. And that blind hen, yes, that turnip-ghost has the confounded cheek to make a proposal, and so on! (*Down R.C. Stuttering. Front to door R.*)

NATALYA STEPANOVNA. What proposal?

CHUBUKOV. Why, he came here so as to propose to you. (*L.*)

NATALYA STEPANOVNA. To propose? To me? Why didn't you tell me so before?

CHUBUKOV. So he dresses up in evening clothes. (*R.C.*) The stuffed sausage! The wizen-faced frump! (*L.*)

NATALYA STEPANOVNA. To propose to me? Ah! (*Falls into an easy chair and wails*) Bring him back! Back! Ah! Bring him here.

CHUBUKOV. Bring whom here?

NATALYA STEPANOVNA. Quick, quick! I'm ill! Fetch him! (*Hysterics*)

CHUBUKOV. What's that? (*To her*) What's the matter with you? (*Clutches at his head*) Oh, unhappy man that I am! I'll shoot myself! I'll hang myself!

NATALYA STEPANOVNA. I'm dying! Fetch him!

CHUBUKOV. At once. Don't yell!

Runs out. A pause. NATALYA STEPANOVNA *wails.*

NATALYA STEPANOVNA. What have they done to me! Fetch him back! Fetch him.

A pause.

CHUBUKOV *runs in. Comes down L.C.*

CHUBUKOV. He's coming, and so on, devil take him! Ouf! Talk to him yourself; I don't want to. (*To R.*)

NATALYA STEPANOVNA. (*Wails*) Fetch him!

CHUBUKOV. (*Yells*) He's coming, I tell you. Oh, what a burden, Lord, to be the father of a grown-up daughter! I'll cut my throat! I will, indeed! (*To her*) We cursed him, abused him, drove him out, and it's all you . . . you!

NATALYA STEPANOVNA. No, it was you!

CHUBUKOV. I tell you it's not my fault. (LOMOV *appears at the door*) Now you talk to him yourself. (*Exit*)

LOMOV *enters, exhausted.*

LOMOV. My heart's palpitating awfully. . . . My foot's gone to sleep. . . . There's something keeps pulling in my side. . . .

NATALYA STEPANOVNA. Forgive us, Ivan Vassilevitch, we were all a little heated. . . . I remember now: Oxen Meadows really are yours.

LOMOV. My heart's beating awfully. . . . My Meadows. . . . My eyebrows are both twitching. . . .

NATALYA STEPANOVNA. The Meadows are yours, yes, yours. . . . Do sit down. . . . (*They sit*) We were wrong. . . .

LOMOV. I did it on principle. . . . My land is worth little to me, but the principle . . .

NATALYA STEPANOVNA. Yes, the principle, just so. . . . Now let's talk of something else.

LOMOV. The more so as I have evidence. My aunt's grandmother gave the land to your father's grandfather's peasants . . .

NATALYA STEPANOVNA. Yes, yes, let that pass. . . . (*Aside*) I wish I knew how to get him started. . . . (*Aloud*) Are you going to start shooting soon?

LOMOV. I'm thinking of having a go at the blackcock, honoured Natalya Stepanovna, after the harvest. Oh, have you heard? Just think, what a misfortune I've had! My dog Guess, whom you know, has gone lame.

NATALYA STEPANOVNA. What a pity! Why?

LOMOV. I don't know. . . . Must have got twisted, or bitten by some other dog. . . . (*Sighs*) My very best dog, to say nothing of the expense. I gave Mironov 125 roubles for him.

NATALYA STEPANOVNA. It was too much, Ivan Vassilevitch.

LOMOV. I think it was very cheap. He's a first-rate dog.

NATALYA STEPANOVNA. Papa gave 85 roubles for his Squeezer, and Squeezer is heaps better than Guess!

LOMOV. Squeezer better than Guess? What an idea! (*Laughs*) Squeezer better than Guess!

NATALYA STEPANOVNA. Of course he's better! Of course, Squeezer is young, he may develop a bit, but on points and pedigree he's better than anything that even Volchanetsky has got.

LOMOV. Excuse me, Natalya Stepanovna, but you forget that he is overshot, and an overshot dog always means the dog is a bad hunter!

NATALYA STEPANOVNA. Overshot, is he? The first time I heard it!

LOMOV. I assure you that his lower jaw is shorter than the upper.

NATALYA STEPANOVNA. Have you measured?

LOMOV. Yes. He's all right at following, of course, but if you want him to get hold of anything . . .

NATALYA STEPANOVNA. In the first place, Squeezer is a thorough-bred animal, the son of Harness and Chisels, while there's no getting at the pedigree of your dog, at all. . . . He's old and as ugly as a worn-out cab-horse.

LOMOV. He is old, but I wouldn't take five Squeezers for him. . . . Why, how can you? Guess is a dog; as for Squeezer, well, it's too funny to argue. . . . Anybody you like has a dog as good as Squeezer . . . you may find them under every bush almost. Twenty-five roubles would be a handsome price to pay for him.

NATALYA STEPANOVNA. There's some demon of contradiction in you today, Ivan Vassilevitch. First you pretend that the Meadows are yours; now, that Guess is better than Squeezer. I don't like people who don't say what they mean, because you know perfectly well that Squeezer is a hundred times better than your silly Guess. Why do you want to say he isn't?

LOMOV. I see, Natalya Stepanovna, that you consider me either blind or a fool. You must realize that Squeezer is overshot!

NATALYA STEPANOVNA. It's not true.

LOMOV. He is!

NATALYA STEPANOVNA. It's not true!

LOMOV. Why shout, madam?

NATALYA STEPANOVNA. Why talk rot? It's awful! It's time your Guess was shot, and you compare him with Squeezer!

LOMOV. Excuse me; I cannot continue this discussion, my heart is palpitating.

NATALYA STEPANOVNA. I've noticed that those hunters argue most who know least.

LOMOV. Madam, please be silent. . . . My heart is going to pieces. . . . (*Shouts*) Shut up!

NATALYA STEPANOVNA. I shan't shut up until you acknowledge that Squeezer is a hundred times better than your Guess!

LOMOV. A hundred times worse! Be hanged to your Squeezer! His head . . . eyes . . . shoulder . . .

NATALYA STEPANOVNA. There's no need to hang your silly Guess; he's half-dead already!

LOMOV. (*Weeps*) Shut up! My heart's bursting!

NATALYA STEPANOVNA. I shan't shut up.

Enter CHUBUKOV.

CHUBUKOV. What's the matter now?

NATALYA STEPANOVNA. Papa, tell us truly, which is the better dog, our Squeezer or his Guess.

LOMOV. Stepan Stepanovitch, I implore you to tell me just one thing; is your Squeezer overshot or not? Yes or no?

CHUBUKOV. And suppose he is? What does it matter? He's the best dog in the district for all that, and so on.

LOMOV. But isn't my Guess better? Really, now?

CHUBUKOV. Don't excite yourself, my precious one. . . . Allow me. . . . Your Guess certainly has his good points. . . . He's pure-bred, firm on his feet, has well-sprung ribs, and all that. But my dear man, if you want to know the truth, that dog has two defects: he's old and he's short in the muzzle.

LOMOV. Excuse me, my heart. . . . Let's take the facts. . . . You will remember that on the Marusinsky hunt my Guess ran neck-and-neck with the Count's dog, while your Squeezer was left a whole verst behind.

CHUBUKOV. He got left behind because the Count's whipper-in hit him with his whip.

LOMOV. And with good reason. The dogs are running after a fox, when Squeezer goes and starts worrying a sheep!

CHUBUKOV. It's not true! . . . My dear fellow, I'm very liable to lose my temper, and so, just because of that, let's stop arguing. You started because everybody is always jealous of everybody else's dogs. Yes, we're all like that! You too, sir, aren't blameless! You no sooner notice that some dog is better than your Guess than you begin with this, that . . . and the other . . . and all that. . . . I remember everything!

LOMOV. I remember too!

CHUBUKOV. (*Teasing him*) I remember, too. . . . What do you re-member?

LOMOV. My heart . . . my foot's gone to sleep. . . . I can't . . .

NATALYA STEPANOVNA. (*Teasing*) My heart. . . . What sort of a hunter are you? You ought to go and lie on the kitchen oven and catch blackbeetles, not go after foxes! My heart!

CHUBUKOV. Yes, really, what sort of a hunter are you, anyway. You ought to sit at home with your palpitations, and not go tracking animals.

You could go hunting, but you only go to argue with people and interfere with their dogs and so on. Let's change the subject in case I lose
my temper. You're not a hunter at all, anyway!

LOMOV. And are you a hunter? You only go hunting to get in with
the Count and to intrigue. . . . Oh, my heart! . . . You're an intriguer!

CHUBUKOV. What? I an intriguer? (*Shouts*) Shut up!

LOMOV. Intriguer!

CHUBUKOV. Boy! Pup!

LOMOV. Old rat!

CHUBUKOV. Shut up or I'll shoot you like a partridge! You fool!

LOMOV. Everybody knows that—oh my heart!—your late wife
used to beat you. . . . My feet . . . temples . . . sparks. . . . I fall,
I fall!

CHUBUKOV. And you're under the slipper of your housekeeper!

LOMOV. There, there, there . . . my heart's burst! My shoulder's
come off. . . . Where is my shoulder? . . . I die. (*Falls into an armchair*) A doctor! (*Faints*)

CHUBUKOV. Boy! Milksop! Fool! I'm sick! (*Drinks water*) Sick!

NATALYA STEPANOVNA. What sort of a hunter are you? You can't
even sit on a horse! (*To her father*) Papa, what's the matter with him?
Papa! Look, papa! (*Screams*) Ivan Vassilevitch! He's dead!

CHUBUKOV. I'm sick! . . . I can't breathe! Air!

NATALYA STEPANOVNA. He's dead. (*Pulls* LOMOV's *sleeve*) Ivan Vassilevitch! Ivan Vassilevitch! What have you done to me? He's dead.
(*Falls into an armchair*) A doctor, a doctor! (*Hysterics*)

CHUBUKOV. Oh! . . . What is it? What's the matter?

NATALYA STEPANOVNA. (*Wails*) He's dead . . . dead!

CHUBUKOV. Who's dead? (*Looks at* LOMOV) So he is! My word!
Water! A doctor! (*Lifts a tumbler to* LOMOV's *mouth*) Drink this! . . .
No, he doesn't drink. . . . It means he's dead, and all that. . . . I'm
the most unhappy of men! Why don't I put a bullet into my brain? Why
haven't I cut my throat yet? What am I waiting for? Give me a knife!
Give me a pistol! (LOMOV *moves*) He seems to be coming round. . . .
Drink some water! That's right. . . .

LOMOV. I see stars . . . mist. . . . Where am I?

CHUBUKOV. Hurry up and get married and—well, to the devil with
you! She's willing! (*He puts* LOMOV's *hand into his daughter's*) She's
willing and all that. I give you my blessing and so on. Only leave me in
peace!

LOMOV. (*Getting up*) Eh? What? To whom?

CHUBUKOV. She's willing! Well? Kiss and be damned to you!

NATALYA STEPANOVNA. (*Wails*) He's alive. . . . Yes, yes, I'm willing. . . .

CHUBUKOV. Kiss each other!

LOMOV. Eh? Kiss whom? (*They kiss*) Very nice, too. Excuse me, what's it all about? Oh, now I understand . . . my heart . . . stars . . . I'm happy. Natalya Stepanovna. . . . (*Kisses her hand*) My foot's gone to sleep.

NATALYA STEPANOVNA. I . . . I'm happy too. . . .

CHUBUKOV. What a weight off my shoulders . . . Ouf!

NATALYA STEPANOVNA. But . . . still you will admit now that Guess is worse than Squeezer.

LOMOV. Better!

NATALYA STEPANOVNA. Worse!

CHUBUKOV. Well, that's a way to start your family bliss! Have some champagne!

LOMOV. He's better!

NATALYA STEPANOVNA. Worse! worse! worse!

CHUBUKOV. (*Trying to shout her down*) Champagne! Champagne!

CURTAIN

THE LONG STAY CUT SHORT,

OR,

THE UNSATISFACTORY SUPPER [1]

by Tennessee Williams

THREE CHARACTERS

BABY DOLL
ARCHIE LEE
AUNT ROSE

THE CURTAIN RISES *on the porch and side yard of a shotgun cottage in Blue Mountain, Mississippi. The frame house is faded and has a greenish-gray cast with dark streaks from the roof, and there are irregularities in the lines of the building. Behind it the dusky cyclorama is stained with the rose of sunset, which is stormy-looking, and the wind has a cat-like whine.*

Upstage from the porch, in the center of the side yard, is a very large rose-bush, the beauty of which is somehow sinister-looking.

A Prokofief sort of music introduces the scene and sets a mood of grotesque lyricism.

The Long Stay Cut Short, or, The Unsatisfactory Supper, printed here in its entirety, provides exercise materials of several different kinds. It may be studied either by an individual actor or by a group for the purpose of analyzing each of the characters, of discovering the meaning of the play as a whole, and of determining the relationship of each character to that total meaning. The dialogue is excellent for practical work in line interpretation. The play may readily be broken into short scenes for study and rehearsal. It may be used in its entirety for rehearsal and performance in class.

The screen door opens with a snarl of rusty springs and latches: this stops the music.

MRS. "BABY DOLL" BOWMAN *appears. She is a large and indolent woman, but her amplitude is not benign, her stupidity is not comfortable. There is a suggestion of Egypt in the arrangement of her glossy black hair and the purple linen dress and heavy brass jewelry that she is wearing.*

ARCHIE LEE BOWMAN *comes out and sucks at his teeth. He is a large man with an unhealthy chalk-white face and slack figure.*

(*The evenly cadenced lines of the dialogue between* BABY DOLL *and* ARCHIE LEE *may be given a singsong reading, somewhat like a grotesque choral incantation, and passages may be divided as strophe and antistrophe by* BABY DOLL'S *movements back and forth on the porch.*)

ARCHIE LEE. The old lady used to could set a right fair table, but not any more. The food has fallen off bad around here lately.

BABY DOLL. You're right about that, Archie Lee. I can't argue with you.

ARCHIE LEE. A good mess of greens is a satisfactory meal if it's cooked with salt-pork an' left on th' stove till it's tender, but thrown in a platter ha'f cooked an' unflavored, it ain't even fit for hog-slops.

BABY DOLL. It's hard t' spoil greens but the old lady sure did spoil 'em.

ARCHIE LEE. How did she manage t' do it?

BABY DOLL. (*Slowly and contemptuously*) Well, she had 'em on th' stove for about an hour. Said she thought they wuh boilin'. I went in the kitchen. The stove was stone-cold. The silly old thing had forgotten to build a fire in it. So I called her back. I said, "Aunt Rose, I think I understand why the greens aren't boilin'." "Why aren't they boilin'?" she says. Well, I told her, "it might have something to do with the fack that the stove issen lighted!"

ARCHIE LEE. What did she say about that?

BABY DOLL. Juss threw back her head an' cackled. "Why, I thought my stove was lighted," she said. "I thought my greens wuh boilin'." Everything is *my*. My stove, my greens, my kitchen. She has taken possession of everything on the place.

ARCHIE LEE. She's getting delusions of grandeur. (*A high, thin laugh is heard inside.*) Why does she cackle that way?

BABY DOLL. How should I know why she cackles! I guess it's supposed to show that she's in a good humor.

ARCHIE LEE. A thing like that can become awf'ly aggravating.

BABY DOLL. It gets on my nerves so bad I could haul off and scream. And obstinate! She's just as obstinate as a mule.

ARCHIE LEE. A person can be obstinate and still cook greens.

BABY DOLL. Not if they're so obstinate they won't even look in a stove t' see if it's lighted.

ARCHIE LEE. Why don't you keep the old lady out of the kitchen?

BABY DOLL. You get me a nigger and I'll keep her out of the kitchen.

The screen door creaks open and AUNT ROSE *comes out on the porch. She is breathless with the exertion of moving from the kitchen, and clings to a porch column while she is catching her breath. She is the type of old lady, about eighty-five years old, that resembles a delicate white-headed monkey. She has on a dress of gray calico which has become too large for her shrunken figure. She has a continual fluttering in her chest which makes her laugh in a witless manner. Neither of the pair on the porch pays any apparent attention to her, though she nods and smiles brightly at each.*

AUNT ROSE. I brought out m' scissors. Tomorrow is Sunday an' I can't stand for my house to be without flowers on Sunday. Besides if we don't cut the roses the wind'll just blow them away.

BABY DOLL. (*Yawns ostentatiously.* ARCHIE LEE *sucks loudly at his teeth.* BABY DOLL, *venting her irritation*) Will you quit suckin' your teeth?

ARCHIE LEE. I got something stuck in my teeth an' I can't remove it.

BABY DOLL. There's such a thing as a tooth-pick made for that purpose.

ARCHIE LEE. I told you at breakfast we didn't have any tooth-picks. I told you the same thing at lunch and the same thing at supper. Does it have to appear in the paper for you to believe it?

BABY DOLL. There's other things with a point besides a tooth-pick.

AUNT ROSE. (*Excitedly*) Archie Lee, son! (*She produces a spool of thread from her bulging skirt-pocket*) You bite off a piece of this thread and run it between your teeth and if that don't dislodge a morsel nothing else will!

ARCHIE LEE. (*Slamming his feet from porch-rail to floor*) Now listen, you all, I want you both to get this. If I want to suck at my teeth, I'm going to suck at my teeth!

AUNT ROSE. That's right, Archie Lee, you go on and suck at your teeth as much as you want to. (BABY DOLL *grunts disgustedly.* ARCHIE

LEE *throws his feet back on the rail and continues sucking loudly at his teeth.* AUNT ROSE, *hesitantly*) Archie Lee, son, you weren't satisfied with your supper. I noticed you left a lot of greens on your plate.

ARCHIE LEE. I'm not strong on greens.

AUNT ROSE. I'm surprised to hear you say that.

ARCHIE LEE. I don't see why you should be. As far as I know I never declared any terrible fondness for greens in your presence, Aunt Rose.

AUNT ROSE. Well, somebody did.

ARCHIE LEE. Somebody probably did sometime and somewhere but that don't mean it was me.

AUNT ROSE. (*With a nervous laugh*) Baby Doll, who is it dotes on greens so much?

BABY DOLL. (*Wearily*) I don't know who dotes on greens, Aunt Rose.

AUNT ROSE. All these likes and dislikes, it's hard to keep straight in your head. But Archie Lee's easy t' cook for, yes, he is, easy t' cook for! Jim's a complainer, oh, my, what a complainer. And Susie's household! What complainers! Every living one of them's a complainer! They're such complainers I die of nervous prostration when I'm cooking for them. But Archie Lee, here, he takes whatever you give him an' seems to love ev'ry bite of it! (*She touches his head*) Bless you, honey, for being so easy t' cook for! (ARCHIE LEE *picks up his chair and moves it roughly away from* AUNT ROSE. *She laughs nervously and digs in her capacious pocket for the scissors*) Now I'm goin' down there an' clip a few roses befo' th' wind blows 'em away 'cause I can't stand my house to be without flowers on Sunday. An' soon as I've finished with that, I'm goin' back in my kitchen an' light up my stove an' cook you some eggs Birmingham. I won't have my men-folks unsatisfied with their supper. Won't have it, I won't stand for it! (*She gets to the bottom of the steps and pauses for breath*)

ARCHIE LEE. What is eggs Birmingham?

AUNT ROSE. Why, eggs Birmingham was Baby Doll's daddy's pet dish.

ARCHIE LEE. That don't answer my question.

AUNT ROSE. (*As though confiding a secret*) I'll tell you how to prepare them.

ARCHIE LEE. I don't care how you prepare them, I just want to know what they are.

AUNT ROSE. (*Reasonably*) Well, son, I can't say what they are without telling how to prepare them. You cut some bread-slices and take the centers out of them. You put the bread-slices in a skillet with butter. Then into each cut-out center you drop one egg and on top of the eggs you put the cut-out centers.

ARCHIE LEE. (*Sarcastically*) Do you build a fire in th' stove?

BABY DOLL. No, you forget to do that. That's why they call them eggs Birmingham, I suppose. (*She laughs at her wit*)

AUNT ROSE. (*Vivaciously*) That's what they call them, they call them eggs Birmingham and Baby Doll's daddy was just insane about them. When Baby Doll's daddy was not satisfied with his supper, he'd call for eggs Birmingham and would stomp his feet on the floor until I'd fixed 'em! (*This recollection seems to amuse her so that she nearly falls over*) He'd stomp his feet on th' floor!—until I'd fixed 'em. . . . (*Her laughter dies out and she wanders away from the porch, examining the scissors*)

BABY DOLL. That old woman is going out of her mind.

ARCHIE LEE. How long is she been with us?

BABY DOLL. She come in October.

ARCHIE LEE. No, it was August. She pulled in here last August.

BABY DOLL. Was it in August? Yes, it was, it was August.

ARCHIE LEE. Why don't she go an' cackle at Susie's awhile?

BABY DOLL. Susie don't have a bed for her.

ARCHIE LEE. Then how about Jim?

BABY DOLL. She was at Jim's direckly before she come here and Jim's wife said she stole from her and that's why she left.

ARCHIE LEE. I don't believe she stole from her. Do you believe she stole from her?

BABY DOLL. I don't believe she stole from her. I think it was just an excuse to get rid of her.

AUNT ROSE *has arrived at the rose-bush. The wind comes up and nearly blows her off her feet. She staggers around and laughs at her precarious balance.*

AUNT ROSE. Oh, my gracious! Ha-ha! Oh! Ha-ha-ha!

BABY DOLL. Why, every time I lay my pocket-book down, the silly old thing picks it up and comes creeping in to me with it, and says, "Count the change."

ARCHIE LEE. What does she do that for?

BABY DOLL. She's afraid I'll accuse her of stealing like Jim's wife did.

AUNT ROSE. (*Singing to herself as she creeps around the rose-bush*)

> Rock of Ages, cleft for me,
> Let me hide myself in thee!

ARCHIE LEE. Your buck-toothed cousin named Bunny, didn't he hit on a new way of using oil-waste?

BABY DOLL. He did an' he didn't.

ARCHIE LEE. That statement don't make sense.

BABY DOLL. Well, you know Bunny. He hits on something and ropes in a few stockholders and then it blows up and the stockholders all go to court. And also he says that his wife's got female trouble.

ARCHIE LEE. They've all got something because they're not mental giants but they've got enough sense to know the old lady is going to break down pretty soon and none of 'em wants it to be while she's on their hands.

BABY DOLL. That is about the size of it.

ARCHIE LEE. And I'm stuck with her?

BABY DOLL. Don't holler.

ARCHIE LEE. I'm nominated the goat!

BABY DOLL. Don't holler, don't holler!

> AUNT ROSE *sings faintly by rose-bush.*

ARCHIE LEE. Then pass the old lady on to one of them others.

BABY DOLL. Which one, Archie Lee?

ARCHIE LEE. Eeny-meeny-miney-mo.—Mo gets her.

BABY DOLL. Which is "Mo"?

ARCHIE LEE. Not me!

Moving slowly and cautiously around the rose-bush with her scissors, AUNT ROSE *sings to herself. Intersperses lines of the hymn with dialogue on porch. A blue dusk is gathering in the yard but a pool of clear light remains upon the rose-bush.*

ARCHIE LEE. (*With religious awe*) Some of them get these lingering types of diseases and have to be given morphine, and they tell me that morphine is just as high as a cat's back.

BABY DOLL. Some of them hang on forever, taking morphine.

ARCHIE LEE. And quantities of it!

BABY DOLL. Yes, they take quantities of it!

ARCHIE LEE. Suppose the old lady broke a hip-bone or something, something that called for morphine!

BABY DOLL. The rest of the folks would have to pitch in and help us.

ARCHIE LEE. Try and extract a dime from your brother Jim! Or Susie or Tom or Bunny! They're all tight as drums, they squeeze ev'ry nickel until th' buffalo bleeds!

BABY DOLL. They don't have much and what they have they hold onto.

ARCHIE LEE. Well, if she does, if she breaks down an' dies on us here, I'm giving you fair warning—(*Lurches heavily to his feet and spits over edge of porch*) I'll have her burned up and her ashes put in an old Coca-cola bottle—(*Flops down again*) Unless your folks kick in with the price of a coffin! (AUNT ROSE *has clipped a few roses. Now she wanders toward the front of the cottage with them*) Here she comes back. Now tell her.

BABY DOLL. Tell her what?

ARCHIE LEE. That she's out-stayed her welcome.

AUNT ROSE. (*Still at some distance*) I want you children to look.

ARCHIE LEE. You going to tell her?

AUNT ROSE. I want you children to look at these poems of nature!

ARCHIE LEE. Or do I have to tell her?

BABY DOLL. You hush up and I'll tell her.

ARCHIE LEE. Then tell her right now, and no more pussy-footing.

AUNT ROSE. (*Now close to the porch*) Look at them, look at them, children, they're poems of nature! (*But the "Children" stare unresponsively, not at the flowers but at* AUNT ROSE'S *face with its extravagant brightness. She laughs uncertainly and turns to* ARCHIE LEE *for a more direct appeal*) Archie Lee, aren't they, aren't they just poems of nature?

He grunts and gets up, and as he passes BABY DOLL'S *chair he gives it a kick to remind her.* BABY DOLL *clears her throat.*

BABY DOLL. (*Uneasily*) Yes, they are poems of nature, Aunt Rose, there is no doubt about it, they are. And, Aunt Rose—while we are talking—step over here for a minute so I can speak to you.

AUNT ROSE *had started away from the porch, as if with a premonition of danger. She stops, her back to the porch, and the fear is visible in her face. It is a familiar fear, one that is graven into her very bones, but which she has never become inured to.*

AUNT ROSE. What is it, honey? (*She turns around slowly*) I know you children are feeling upset about something. It don't take a Gypsy with cards to figure that out. You an' Archie Lee both are upset about something. I think you were both unsatisfied with your supper. Isn't that it, Baby Doll? The greens didn't boil long enough. Don't you think I know that? (*She looks from* BABY DOLL'S *face to* ARCHIE LEE'S *back with a hesitant laugh*) I played a fool trick with my stove, I thought it was lighted and all that time it was . . .

BABY DOLL. Aunt Rose, won't you set down so we can talk comfortably?

AUNT ROSE. (*With a note of hysteria*) I don't want to set down, I don't want to set down, I can talk on my feet! I tell you, getting up an' down is more trouble than it's worth! Now what is it, honey? As soon as I've put these in water, I'm going to light up my stove an' cook you two children some eggs Birmingham. Archie Lee, son, you hear that?

ARCHIE LEE. (*Roughly, his back still turned*) I don't want eggs Birmingham.

BABY DOLL. He don't want eggs Birmingham and neither do I. But while we are talking, Aunt Rose—well—Archie Lee's wondered and I've been wondering, too . . .

AUNT ROSE. About what, Baby Doll?

BABY DOLL. Well, as to whether or not you've—made any plans.

AUNT ROSE. Plans?

BABY DOLL. Yes, plans.

AUNT ROSE. What kind of plans, Baby Doll?

BABY DOLL. Why, plans for the future, Aunt Rose.

AUNT ROSE. Oh! Future! No—no, when an old maid gets to be nearly a hundred years old, the future don't seem to require much planning for, honey. Many's a time I've wondered but I've never doubted. . . . (*Her voice dies out and there is a strain of music as she faces away from the porch*) I'm not forgotten by Jesus! No, my Sweet Savior has not forgotten about me! The time isn't known to me or to you, Baby Doll, but it's known by Him and when it comes He will call me. A wind'll come down and lift me an' take me away! The way that it will the roses when they're like I am. . . . (*The music dies out and she turns back to the tribunal on the front porch*)

BABY DOLL. (*Clearing her throat again*) That's all very well, Aunt Rose, to trust in Jesus, but we've got to remember that Jesus only helps those that—well—help themselves!

AUNT ROSE. Oh, I know that, Baby Doll! (*She laughs*) Why, I learned that in my cradle, I reckon I must have learned that before I was born. Now when have I ever been helpless? I could count my sick days, the days that I haven't been up and around, on my fingers! My Sweet Savior has kept me healthy an' active, active an' healthy, yes, I do pride myself on it, my age hasn't made me a burden! And when the time comes that I have to lean on His shoulder, I —

ARCHIE LEE *turns about roughly.*

ARCHIE LEE. All this talk about Jesus an' greens didn't boil an' so forth has got nothing to do with the situation! Now look here, Aunt Rose —

BABY DOLL. (*Getting up*) Archie Lee, will you hold your tongue for a minute?

ARCHIE LEE. Then you talk up! And plain! What's there to be so pussy-footing about?

BABY DOLL. There's ways and there's ways of talking anything over!

ARCHIE LEE. Well, talk it over and get off the subject of Jesus! There's Susie, there's Jim, there's Tom and Jane and there's Bunny! And if none of them suits her, there's homes in the county will take her! Just let her decide on which one she is ready to visit. First thing in the morning I'll pile her things in the car and drive her out to whichever one's she's decided! Now ain't that a simple procedure compared to all of this pussy-footing around? Aunt Rose has got sense. She's counted the rooms in this house! She knows that I'm nervous, she knows that I've got work to do and a workingman's got to be fed! And his house is his house and he wants it the way that he wants it! Well, Jesus Almighty, if that's not a plain, fair and square way of settling the matter, I'll wash my hands clean and leave you two women to talk it over yourselves! Yes, I'll—be God damned if—!

He rushes in and slams the screen door. There is a long pause in which BABY DOLL *looks uncomfortably at nothing, and* AUNT ROSE *stares at the screen door.*

AUNT ROSE. (*Finally*) I thought you children were satisfied with my cooking.

A blue dusk has gathered in the yard. AUNT ROSE *moves away from the porch and there is a strain of music. The music is drowned out by the cat-like whine of the wind turning suddenly angry.* BABY DOLL *gets up from her wicker chair.*

BABY DOLL. Archie Lee, Archie Lee, you help me in with these chairs before they blow over! (*She drags her chair to the screen door*) It looks and sounds like a twister! Hold that screen open for me! Pull in that chair! Now this one! We better get down in the cellar! (*As an after-thought*) Aunt Rose, come in here so we can shut this door!

AUNT ROSE *shakes her head slightly. Then she looks toward the sky, above and beyond the proscenium, where something portentous is forming.*

> BABY DOLL. (*Back in the house*) Call Aunt Rose in!
> ARCHIE LEE. (*Near the door*) The stubborn old thing won't budge.

The door slams shut. The whine of the angry cat turns into a distant roar and the roar approaches. But AUNT ROSE *remains in the yard, her face still somberly but quietly thoughtful. The loose gray calico of her dress begins to whip and tug at the skeleton lines of her figure. She looks wonderingly at the sky, then back at the house beginning to shrink into darkness, then back at the sky from which the darkness is coming, at each with the same unflinching but troubled expression. Nieces and nephews and cousins, like pages of an album, are rapidly turned through her mind, some of them loved as children but none of them really her children and all of them curiously unneedful of the devotion that she had offered so freely, as if she had always carried an armful of roses that no one had ever offered a vase to receive. The flimsy gray scarf is whipped away from her shoulders. She makes an awkward gesture and sinks to her knees. Her arms let go of the roses. She reaches vaguely after them. One or two she catches. The rest blow away. She struggles back to her feet. The blue dusk deepens to purple and the purple to black and the roar comes on with the force of a locomotive as* AUNT ROSE'S *figure is still pushed toward the rose-bush.*

THE CURTAIN FALLS

Bibliography

These books, dealing either wholly or in part with the problems of the actor, will provide informative and interesting reading.

Barrault, Jean-Louis, *Reflections on the Theatre*, translated by Barbara Wall. London: Rockliff, 1951.

A stimulating commentary upon theatre and theatre practice, with many specific references to acting, by one of the most idealistic as well as one of the most successful actor-directors of the modern stage.

Boleslavsky, Richard, *Acting: The First Six Lessons*. New York: Theatre Arts Books, 1933.

A small and valuable book for the beginning actor. It consists of six dialogues on Concentration, Memory of Emotion, Dramatic Action, Characterization, Observation, and Rhythm.

Chekhov, Michael, *To the Actor*. New York: Harper & Brothers, Publishers, 1953.

A creative approach to acting by a student of Stanislavski and a former member of the Moscow Art Theatre. The concepts, especially those related to the "Psychological Gesture," are imaginative. The exercises are stimulating and practical, providing excellent problems in Improvisation.

Cole, Toby, ed., *Acting: A Handbook of the Stanislavski Method*. New York: Lear Publishers, Inc., 1947.

A group of articles describing principles and practices based upon the work of Stanislavski. I. Rapoport, "The Work of the Actor," is particularly useful.

Cole, Toby, and Helen Krich Chenoy, eds., *Actors on Acting*. New York: Crown Publishers, 1949.

A splendid selection of significant materials on the art of acting from Plato to José Ferrer and Howard Lindsay.

Duerr, Edwin, *Radio and Television Acting*. New York: Rinehart & Company, Inc., 1950.

An account of general principles of acting and their adaptation to the requirements of radio and television. Provides ample and excellent materials for practice.

Eustis, Morton, *Players at Work*. New York: Theatre Arts Books, 1937.

A series of interviews with some important modern actors about their methods of work. Among those interviewed are Alfred Lunt, Lynn Fontanne, Helen Hayes, Alla Nazimova, Burgess Meredith.

Jones, Margo, *Theatre-in-the-Round*. New York: Rinehart & Company, Inc., 1951.

The story of the most outstandingly successful arena theatre in America, containing many references to the problems of acting on the arena stage.

Redgrave, Michael, *The Actor's Ways and Means*. London: William Heinemann, Ltd., 1953.

A series of Rockefeller Foundation Lectures delivered before the Department of Drama, University of Bristol. An important modern actor of stage and screen discusses the problems of his art. In a lecture on "Instinct and Method" he considers the practicability of some of Stanislavski's principles.

Seyler, Athene, and Stephen Haggard, *The Craft of Comedy*. New York: Theatre Arts Books, 1946.

Expert advice on the acting of comedy.

Stanislavski, Constantin, *An Actor Prepares*, translated by Elizabeth Reynolds Hapgood. New York: Theatre Arts Books, 1936.

The most widely read of Stanislavski's works. It sets forth the basic principles of the "inner technique" of acting and describes the concepts of Sensory Recall, Emotion Memory, Relaxation, Circles of Concentration, Communion, Adaptation, Through Line of Action, and so forth.

————, *Building a Character*, translated by Elizabeth Reynolds Hapgood. New York: Theatre Arts Books, 1949.

This book is less widely known than *An Actor Prepares*, but it is vitally important to an understanding of Stanislavski's principles.

It is concerned primarily with problems of making a character effective on the stage. It is a necessary supplement to the earlier work.

Stanislavski, Constantin, *My Life in Art*, translated by J. J. Robbins. New York: Theatre Arts Books, 1948.

Stanislavski's autobiography and an account of the founding and working methods of the Moscow Art Theatre.

Young, Stark, *Theatre Practice*. New York: Charles Scribner's Sons, 1926.

A rewarding series of articles by one of the outstanding critics of the American theatre.

Index

Index

173